RHYMING DICTIONARY

A POCKET REFERENCE GUIDE FOR ALL WRITERS

HAL•LEONARD®

ISBN 978-1-4234-9970-1

HAL•LEONARD®
CORPORATION
7777 W. BLUEMOUND RD. P.O. BOX 13819 MILWAUKEE, WI 53213

In Australia contact:
Hal Leonard Australia Pty. Ltd.
4 Lentara Court
Cheltenham, Victoria, 3192 Australia
Email: ausadmin@halloonard.com.au

Visit Hal Leonard Online at
www.halleonard.com

CONTENTS

FOREWORD

One of the most useful and unique resources available to all writers is a book such as this. In addition to your own imagination and rhyming skills, the *Rhyming Dictionary* is a must for writers. It is a powerful tool when you are just flat stumped for a word. I personally utilize lots of triple-rhyming schemes, such as the chorus of "Everlasting Love," which I co-wrote with Mac Gayden. In this type of rhyming, as well as others, this book will provide you with a creative advantage as you uncover exciting words that will enhance your work.

Today's "world of words" is ever-changing and more expressive than ever. This book's collection of 30,000 words, including proper nouns and popular expressions, will be most helpful. The next time I pick up my guitar and sit down to write, I'll have the *Rhyming Dictionary* handy.

Enjoy!
Buzz Cason

INTRODUCTION

Designed with today's songwriter/lyricist in mind, the *Rhyming Dictionary* is an efficient, concise, and user-friendly resource of some 30,000 words; a contemporary lexicon that encompasses standard vocabulary, proper names (common, place, literary, mythological), popular expressions, and for the sake of range and variety, some lesser-known and esoteric terms. Rather than following the "common spelling" format found in most rhyming dictionaries, the entries of this book have been organized alpha-phonetically, to both maximize word choice and minimize cross-referencing.

The alpha-phonetic structure, in which words are grouped according to the vowel sound of their final (or only) syllable, allocates all words that rhyme exactly—as well as those that rhyme closely—to the same section. (See the "Pronunciation Guide" and "How to Use This Book" on the following pages.) By segmenting all phonetically compatible words together, rather than scattering them throughout the book according to their common spelling, the user will not only be able to readily locate a desired exact rhyme, but may peruse the consecutive pages of phonetically attuned options for alternative word choices. And because the inventive imagination of the present-day lyricist is seldom devoted to, and often restricted by, the limitations inherent in exact rhymes, the range of rhyming options provided in this book is sure to stimulate and facilitate the creative process itself.

Intended to serve the specific needs of modern songwriter/lyricist, the *Rhyming Dictionary* is also ideal for the writer, poet, or recreational rhymester who seeks a convenient and comprehensive source of word selection and poetic inspiration.

PRONUNCIATION GUIDE

Phonetic Vowel Sounds

aa	r*a*t		i	r*i*p
ah	r*o*t		oh	r*o*pe
aw	r*aw*		oo	r*oo*m
ay	r*ay*		ow	r*ou*nd
ee	r*ea*p		oy	r*oi*l
eh	r*e*d		uh	r*u*t*
ei	r*i*pe		uu	r*oo*k

*only slightly stressed in multisyllabic words: wa*ff*le, nox*iou*s, ea*ge*r.

Vowel Sounds Colored by Subsequent "r"

ahr	b*ar*		ohr	b*oar*
ehr	b*ear*		uhr	b*urr*
ir	b*eer*		uur	b*oor*

Special Phonetic Consonant Sounds

ch	wa*tch*, fu*t*ure		ns	se*ns*e, ce*nts*
f	cou*gh*, gly*ph*, mu*ff*le		th	brea*the*, fea*th*er
g	dra*g*, bo*gg*le		thh	brea*th*, pan*th*er
j	messa*g*e, stran*g*er		s	p*s*yche, Cir*c*e
k	stoi*c*, ar*ch*eology		sh	wi*sh*, con*sc*ious
ks	fo*x*, e*x*tra		z	guitar*s*, co*s*mos
ng	waiti*ng*, a*n*chor		zh	entoura*g*e, mea*s*ure
nk	i*nk*, spelu*nk*er		zm	cha*sm*, pri*sm*

HOW TO USE THIS BOOK

There are three levels of organization to the alpha-phonetic format used herein to ensure that words with the greatest phonetic compatibility are within the closest proximity.

> Level 1—comprised of words with final (or only) syllables ending in the *phonetic vowel sound* plus any ending consonants (i.e., **–uh**, **–uhb**, **–uhd**, etc.). These are listed alphabetically, with consideration to the *special phonetic consonant sounds* (see Pronunciation Guide).
>
> Level 2—comprised of words that share the Level 1 syllable plus one or two preceding syllables. These are listed alphabetically by the *preceding* syllable (i.e., **–ee-uhn**, **–ehr-uhn**, **–ei-uhn**, etc.).
>
> Level 3—comprised of words that share a Level 1 syllable *augmented* by a leading consonant (i.e., **–buhn**, **–chuhn**, **–duhn**, etc.). These words are listed alphabetically first *by the ending syllable*, and secondly *by the preceding syllable* (i.e., **–i-buhn**, **–uhr-buhn**, **–ohr-chuhn**, **–uhn-chuhn**, etc.).

To assist those users seeking words of a specific meter (number of syllables), each word group is preceded by a *meter marker* (i.e. (1), (2), (3), etc.), which indicates the number of syllables found in each subsequent word.

Also, in the interest of space so precious in a pocket-sized volume, words created by the augmentation of a root form listed herein (with common suffixes such as *-s*, *-ed*, *-est*, *-ing*, *-ness*, etc.) have not been listed, but are suggested at the end of the applicable phonetic grouping.

–aab

(1) blab, cab, crab, dab, drab, gab, grab, jab, lab, nab, scab, slab, stab, tab. (2) Ahab, Punjab, Skylab. (3) taxicab.

–aach

(1) batch, catch, hatch, latch, match, patch, scratch, snatch, thatch.
(2) attach, detach, dispatch, mismatch, potlatch, unlatch.

–aad

(1) ad, add, bad, brad, cad, Chad, clad, dad, fad, gad, glad, grad, had, lad, mad, pad, plaid, sad, shad, tad. (2) Baghdad, footpad, gonad, monad, nomad, Sinbad, tetrad, unclad. (3) Galahad, hanging chad, Iliad, iron-clad, Trinidad, undergrad, Olympiad.

–ei-aad

(2) dryad, dyad, naiad, triad. (4) jeremiad.

–aadj

(1) badge, cadge, hajj, Madge.

–aaf

(1) calf, chaff, gaff, graph, half, laugh, quaff, staff. (2) behalf, carafe, distaff, Falstaff, flagstaff, Flagstaff, giraffe, pikestaff, riff-raff, seraph. (3) autograph, better half, epitaph, half-and-half, lithograph, monograph, paragraph, phonograph, photograph, polygraph, quarterstaff, telegraph.

–aaft

(1) aft, craft, daft, draft, draught, graft, haft, raft, shaft, Taft. (2) aircraft, spacecraft, stagecraft, statecraft, witchcraft, handicraft, overdraft, watercraft.
ALSO: –aaf + -ed (i.e., *graphed*, *photographed*).

–aag

(1) ag, bag, brag, crag, drag, fag, flag, gag, hag, Hague, jag, lag, nag, plague, quag, rag, sag, shag, slag, snag, stag, swag, tag, vague, wag.
(2) dishrag, grab bag, ragtag, sandbag, zigzag. (3) saddlebag, scalawag.

–aak

(1) ach, back, black, clack, claque, crack, hack, jack, Jack, knack, lack, Mac, pack, plaque, quack, rack, sac, sack, shack, slack, smack, snack, stack, tack, thwack, track, whack, wrack, yak. (2) aback, alack, arrack, attack, bareback, bivouac, blackjack, bootblack, cognac, drawback, gimcrack, haystack, hogback, horseback, humpback, hunchback, Iraq, kayak, Kodak, knick-knack, macaque, Muzak, Prozac, ransack, repack, rucksack, Shadrach, shellac, Slovak, tic-tac, unpack, zwieback. (3) almanac, applejack, bric-a-brac, Cadillac, cardiac, cul-de-sac, Fond du Lac, Hackensack, haversack, iliac, ipecac, maniac, piggyback, Pontiac, stickleback, tamarack, zodiac. (4) ammoniac, demoniac, elegiac. (5) aphrodisiac, hypochondriac, kleptomaniac, pyromaniac, sacroiliac.

–aakt

(1) act, bract, fact, pact, tact, tract. (2) abstract, attract, compact, contact, detract, diffract, distract, enact, exact, extract, impact, infract, intact, protract, react, redact, refract, retract, subtract, transact. (3) artifact, cataract, counteract, interact, overact, re-enact, retroact, subcompact. (4) ammoniac, demoniac, elegiac. (5) matter-of-fact, overreact.
ALSO: –aak + -ed (i.e., *hacked, shellacked*).

–ahn-traakt

(2) contract, entr'acte.

–aaks

(1) ax, fax, flax, lax, Max, sax, tax, wax. (2) addax, Ajax, anthrax, climax, relax, syntax. (3) battleaxe, Halifax, parallax. (4) Adirondacks, anticlimax.

–ohr-aaks

(2) borax, storax, thorax.

–aal

(1) Al, Hal, pal, Sal, shall. (2) banal, canal, corral, locale, morale. (3) bacchanal, femme fatale, musicale, rationale. (4) Guadalcanal.

–aalp

(1) Alp, scalp.

–aalv

(1) salve, valve. (2) bivalve. (3) univalve.

–aam

(1) am, bam, cam, clam, cram, dam, damn, dram, graham, Graham, gram, ham, jam, jamb, lam, lamb, ma'am, Pam, pram, ram, Sam, scram, sham, slam, spam, Spam, swam, tram, wham, yam. (2) exam, flim-flam, iamb, logjam, madam, program, Siam. (3) Abraham, Amsterdam, Birmingham, anagram, cablegram, cryptogram, diagram, diaphragm, dithyramb, epigram, monogram, Rotterdam, Surinam, telegram, Uncle Sam. (4) radiogram. (5) parallelogram.

–aamp

(1) amp, camp, champ, clamp, cramp, damp, lamp, ramp, scamp, stamp, tamp, tramp, vamp. (2) decamp, encamp, firedamp. (3) afterdamp. (4) kerosene lamp.

–aan

(1) an, Ann, Anne, ban, bran, can, clan, Dan, fan, Fran, Jan, Klan, man, Nan, pan, Pan, plan, ran, scan, span, tan, than, van. (2) afghan, Afghan, Batman, began, Cheyenne, demesne, dishpan, divan, foreran, he-man, Iran, Japan, Koran, Milan, pecan, Qu'ran, rattan, sedan, trepan, unman. (3) caravan, middleman, minuteman, overran, Pakistan, Peter Pan, spick-and-span, Spider-man, Superman, Yucatan. (4) Afghanistan, catamaran.

–aanch

(1) blanch, Blanche, branch, ranch, stanch. (2) carte blanche. (3) avalanche.

–aand

(1) and, band, bland, brand, gland, grand, hand, land, sand, stand, strand. (2) backhand, command, demand, disband, dreamland, expand, fore-hand, Greenland, Iceland, remand, Rhineland, unhand, withstand. (3) ampersand, contraband, countermand, dairyland, fairyland, fatherland, firebrand, four-in-hand, hinterland, Holy Land, motherland, overland, reprimand, Rio Grande, underhand, understand, wonderland. (4) misunderstand, multiplicand.

–aand-staand

(2) bandstand, grandstand, handstand.

–aang

(1) bang, bhang, clang, fang, gang, gangue, hang, pang, rang, sang, slang, sprang, tang, twang, yang. (2) harangue, meringue, mustang, she-bang. (3) boomerang, yin and yang.

–aank

(1) bank, blank, clank, crank, dank, drank, flank, franc, frank, Frank, hank, Hank, lank, plank, prank, rank, sank, shank, shrank, spank, stank, swank, tank, thank, yank, Yank. (2) embank, outflank, outrank, point-blank, snowbank. (3) Mountebank.

–aankt

(3) sacrosanct.
ALSO: **–aank** + -ed (i.e., *banked, outranked*).

–aans (–aants)

(1) chance, dance, France, glance, lance, manse, prance, stance, trance. (2) advance, askance, bechance, enhance, entrance, expanse, finance, last dance, mischance, Penzance, perchance, romance. (3) circumstance.

–aant

(1) ant, aunt, can't, cant, chant, grant, Grant, pant, plant, rant, scant, shan't, slant. (2) aslant, decant, descant, enchant, extant, gallant, implant. (3) adamant, disenchant, gallivant.

–aap

(1) cap, chap, clap, flap, gap, hap, Jap, lap, map, nap, pap, rap, sap, scrap, slap, snap, strap, tap, trap, wrap, yap. (2) backslap, burlap, catnap, claptrap, dunce cap, entrap, enwrap, foolscap, kidnap, lagniappe, mad-cap, mayhap, mishap, nightcap, recap, shrink-wrap, skullcap, skycap, snowcap, unwrap. (3) handicap, overlap, rattletrap, thunderclap.

–aaps

(1) apse, lapse. (2) collapse, elapse, perhaps, relapse, synapse, time-lapse.
ALSO: **–aap** + -s (i.e., *snaps, kidnaps*).

–aapt

(1) apt, rapt. (2) adapt.
ALSO: **–aap** + -ed (i.e., *clapped, entrapped*).

–aas

(1) ass, bass, brass, class, crass, gas, glass, grass, lass, mass, pass.
(2) alas, Alsace, amass, bluegrass, crevasse, first-class, high-class, impasse, low-class, surpass, third-class. (3) demitasse, fiberglass, gallowglass, Hallowmas, hippocras, isinglass, lemongrass, looking glass, middle-class, overpass, sassafras, underpass.

–uh-raas

(2) harass, morass.

–aash

(1) ash, bash, brash, cache, cash, clash, crash, dash, flash, gash, gnash, hash, lash, mash, Nash, plash, rash, sash, slash, smash, splash, thrash, trash. (2) abash, mishmash, moustache, panache, Wabash. (3) balder-dash, calabash, succotash.

–aask

(1) ask, bask, Basque, cask, flask, mask, masque, Pasch, task.
(2) unmask.

–aasp

(1) asp, clasp, gasp, grasp, hasp, rasp. (2) unclasp.

–aast

(1) blast, cast, caste, fast, hast, last, mast, past, vast. (2) aghast, Belfast, bombast, broadcast, contrast, forecast, gymnast, miscast, newscast, outcast, repast, steadfast, typecast, webcast. (3) flabbergast, overcast, simulcast, telecast. (4) ecclesiast, enthusiast, iconoclast.
ALSO: –aas + -ed (i.e., *passed, harassed*).

–aat

(1) at, bat, brat, cat, chat, fat, flat, gnat, hat, mat, Matt, Nat, pat, Pat, phat, plat, rat, sat, slat, spat, sprat, stat, tat, that, vat. (2) cravat, muskrat, polecat, whereat. (3) acrobat, automat, butterfat, copycat, diplomat, habitat, hemostat, photostat, thermostat, tit for tat, vampire bat. (4) Jehoshaphat, mortal combat.

–ahm-baat

(2) combat, wombat.

–uh-kraat

(3) autocrat, bureaucrat, democrat, plutocrat. (4) aristocrat.

–aav

(1) calve, halve, have, salve.

–aaz

(1) as, has, jazz, razz, spaz. (2) pizzazz, topaz, whereas. (3) Alcatraz, razzmatazz.

–aazm (–aa-zuhm)

(2) chasm, spasm. (3) orgasm, phantasm, sarcasm. (4) cataplasm, pleonasm, protoplasm. (5) enthusiasm, iconoclasm.

–ahb

(1) blob, bob, Bob, cob, Cobb, fob, glob, gob, hob, job, knob, lob, mob, rob, Rob, sob, slob, snob, squab, swab, throb. (2) corncob, heartthrob, hobnob, kabob, macabre, nabob. (4) thingamabob.

–ahch

(1) blotch, botch, crotch, notch, scotch, Scotch, splotch, swatch, watch. (2) deathwatch, debauch, hopscotch, hotchpotch, stopwatch, topnotch, wristwatch.

–ahd

(1) clod, cod, god, God, nod, odd, plod, pod, prod, quad, rod, Rod, scrod, shod, sod, squad, Todd, trod, wad. (2) ballade, Cape Cod, couvades, façade, jihad, nimrod, roughshod, roulade, slipshod, unshod. (3) demigod, goldenrod, promenade. (4) Scheherazade.

–ahj

(1) dodge, lodge. (2) dislodge, hodgepodge.

–ahk

(1) Bach, Bloch, block, bock, chock, clock, cock, crock, doc, dock, flock, frock, hock, jock, knock, loch, lock, Mach, mock, pock, roc, rock, shock, smock, sock, stock. (2) ad hoc, Balzac, Bangkok, deadlock, fetlock, Hancock, hemlock, padlock, peacock, petcock, pet rock, Rorschach, shamrock, Sherlock, tick-tock, unfrock, unlock, woodcock. (3) alpenstock, antilock, Antioch, hollyhock, Little Rock, Offenbach, poppycock, shuttlecock, weathercock.

–aa-**dahk**

(2) haddock, paddock, shaddock.

–ehd-**lahk**

(2) deadlock, dreadlock, headlock, wedlock.

–aa-**sahk**

(2) cassock, hassock.

–**ahks**

(1) box, fox, lox, ox, phlox, pox, sox, vox. (2) bandbox, hatbox, icebox, mailbox, postbox, smallpox, soapbox, Xerox. (3) chickenpox, equinox, orthodox, paradox. (4) heterodox, penalty box, unorthodox.
ALSO: –**ahk** + -*s* (i.e., *blocks*, *shamrocks*).

–**ahkt**

(2) concoct, decoct, entr'acte, shell-shocked.
ALSO: –**ahk** + -*ed* (i.e., *clocked*, *deadlocked*).

–**ahl**

(1) doll, loll, moll. (2) atoll, banal. (3) bacchanal.

-**ahlm**

(1) balm, calm, palm, psalm, qualm. (2) becalm, embalm.

-**ahlmz**

(1) alms.
ALSO: –**ahlm** + -*s* (i.e., *calms*, *embalms*).

–**ahlv**

(1) solve. (2) absolve, convolve, devolve, evolve, involve, resolve, revolve.

–**ahm**

(1) bomb, Dom, Guam, mom, prom, rhomb, ROM, Tom. (2) aplomb, Madame, pompom, salaam, step-mom.

–**ahmp**

(1) comp, pomp, romp, swamp.

–**ahmpt**

(1) prompt, romped, swamped.
(3) contretemps.

–ahn

(1) con, don, John, on, swan, wan, yon. (2) anon, argon, Aswan, Bay-onne, bonbon, Ceylon, chiffon, cretonne, hands-on, head-on, hereon, icon, neutron, odds-on, proton, Teflon, thereon, turned-on, upon, walk-on, whereon, Yvonne. (3) Amazon, antiphon, Aragon, Avalon, colo-phon, decagon, deuteron, echelon, electron, epsilon, helicon, hexagon, lexicon, marathon, mastodon, myrmidon, nonagon, Oberon, octagon, omicron, Oregon, paragon, parmesan, Parthenon, pentagon, polygon, Rubicon, silicon, synchrotron, tarragon, upsilon. (4) Agamemnon, phenomenon, Saskatchewan, (5) prolegomenon.

–ee-ahn

(2) eon, Leon, neon, paean, peon. (3) pantheon.

–ei-lahn

(2) nylon, pylon.

–ahnch

(1) conch. (2) carte blanche.

–ahnd

(1) blond, blonde, bond, conned, donned, fond, frond, pond, wand.
(2) abscond, beyond, despond, respond. (3) correspond, demimonde, vagabond.

–ahns

(1) Hans, nonce, sconce. (2) ensconce, response, séance. (3) ambience, renaissance. (4) insouciance, par excellence.

–ahnt

(1) font, Kant, want. (2) croissant, Piedmont, savant, Vermont. (3) au courant, bon vivant, commandant, confidant, debutante, dénouement, dilettante, en passant, restaurant, sycophant. (4) accouchement, accou-trement, hierophant.

–ahp

(1) bop, chop, cop, crop, drop, flop, fop, hop, lop, mop, plop, pop, prop, shop, slop, sop, stop, strop, swap, top. (2) Aesop, atop, co-op, dewdrop, eavesdrop, flip-flop, snowdrop, tiptop, workshop. (3) barbershop, lol-lipop, whistle stop.

–ahpt

(1) opt. (2) adopt.
ALSO: **–ahp** + -ed (i.e., *swapped, eavesdropped*).

–ahr

(1) are, bar, car, char, czar, far, jar, mar, noire, par, scar, spar, star, tar, tsar. (2) afar, agar, ajar, all-star, armoire, bazaar, bizarre, catarrh, cigar, Dakar, debar, disbar, feldspar, guitar, hussar, Navarre, pourboire, rebar, sitar. (3) Alcazar, au revoir, avatar, bête noire, caviar, cinnabar, regis-trar, repertoire, reservoir, samovar, seminar, superstar, VCR, Zanzibar. (4) agar-agar, crepuscular.

–ahrb

(1) Barb, garb. (2) rhubarb.

-ahrch

(1) arch, larch, march, March, parch, starch. (2) outmarch. (3) countermarch.

–ahrf

(1) arf, barf, scarf.

–ahrj

(1) barge, charge, large, Marge, serge. (2) discharge, enlarge, recharge, surcharge. (3) overcharge, supercharge, undercharge.

–ahrk

(1) arc, ark, bark, cark, Clark, Clarke, dark, hark, lark, mark, Mark, park, sark, shark, spark, stark. (2) aardvark, Bismarck, debark, embark, landmark, Petrarch, remark, skylark, tanbark, trademark. (3) cutty sark, disembark, hierarch, matriarch, meadowlark, Noah's Ark, oligarch, patriarch.

–ahrl

(1) Carl, gnarl, marl, snarl.

–ahrm

(1) arm, charm, farm, harm, marm. (2) alarm, disarm, forearm, gendarme, schoolmarm, strong-arm, unarm.

–ahrn

(1) barn, darn, tarn, yarn.

–ahrp

(1) carp, harp, scarp, sharp, tarp. (2) cardsharp, escarp, mouth harp.
(3) autoharp, counterscarp, pericarp.

–ahrs

(1) arse, farce, parse, sparse.

–ahrsh

(1) harsh, marsh.

–ahrt

(1) art, Art, Bart, cart, chart, dart, fart, hart, heart, jart, mart, part, smart, start, tart. (2) apart, depart, Descartes, impart, outsmart, pushcart, rampart, sweetheart, upstart. (3) à la carte, apple cart, counterpart, heart-to-heart.

–ahrthh

(1) Garth, hearth.

–ahrv

(1) carve, starve.

–ahrz

(1) Mars.
ALSO: **–ahr** + *-s* (i.e., *bars*, *cigars*).

–ahs

(2) bathos, pathos.

–ahsh

(1) bosh, gosh, gouache, josh, posh, quash, slosh, squash, swash, wash.
(2) awash, b'gosh, galosh, goulash, Oshkosh. (3) mackintosh.

–aht

(1) blot, clot, cot, dot, Dot, got, grot, hot, jot, knot, lot, not, plot, pot, rot, Scot, Scott, shot, slot, snot, sot, spot, squat, tot, trot, watt, what, yacht. (2) allot, begot, besot, big shot, bloodshot, boycott, cocotte, Crock-Pot, culotte, dogtrot, ergot, forgot, foxtrot, fylfot, gavotte, kumquat, loquat, slipknot, somewhat, unknot. (3) aliquot, apricot, bergamot, Camelot, caveat, counterplot, diddley-squat, Huguenot, Lancelot, ocelot, patriot, polyglot, tommyrot, undershot. (4) forget-me-not.

–aak-**paht**

(2) crackpot, jackpot.

–ahthh

(1) Goth. (3) Ostrogoth, Visigoth.

–ahz

(1) Oz, vase, was. (2) Cray Paz, La Paz.
ALSO: –ah + -s (i.e., *blahs*, *cha chas*).

–ahzh

(2) Belle Age, barrage, collage, corsage, garage, ménage, mirage.

(3) arbitrage, badinage, bon voyage, camouflage, curettage, decoupage, entourage, fuselage, persiflage. (4) espionage.

–aw

(1) awe, caw, chaw, claw, craw, draw, faugh, flaw, gnaw, haw, jaw, law, maw, paw, pshaw, raw, saw, Shaw, squaw, straw, taw, thaw, yaw. (2) coleslaw, cumshaw, foresaw, gewgaw, guffaw, heehaw, jackdaw, jigsaw, macaw, paw-paw, rickshaw, seesaw, southpaw, Warsaw, withdraw. (3) Arkansas, contretemps, mackinaw, Omaha, overawe.

–awd

(1) bawd, broad, Claude, fraud, gaud, laud, Maude. (2) abroad, applaud, defraud, maraud.
ALSO: –aw + -ed (i.e., *awed*, *guffawed*).

–awf

(1) cough, doff, off, scoff, soph, trough. (2) Chekhov, Khrushchev, take-off. (3) Gorbachev, Molotov.

–awft

(1) croft, loft, oft, soft. (2) aloft, hayloft. (3) undercroft.
ALSO: –awf + -ed (i.e., *doffed*, *scoffed*).

–awg

(1) bog, clog, cog, dog, flog, fog, frog, grog, hog, jog, log, nog, Prague, slog. (2) agog, bulldog, eggnog, warthog. (3) analogue, catalogue, captain's log, Decalogue, demagogue, dialogue, epilogue, monologue, pedagogue, pettifog, synagogue, travelogue.

-awk

(1) auk, balk, caulk, chalk, gawk, hawk, squawk, stalk, talk, walk.
(2) boardwalk, catwalk, Mohawk. (3) belle époque, double talk, tomahawk. (4) Bela Bartok, Manitowoc. (5) Oconomowoc.

-awl

(1) all, awl, ball, brawl, call, crawl, drawl, fall, gall, Gaul, hall, haul, mall, maul, pall, Paul, pawl, Saul, scrawl, shawl, small, sprawl, squall, stall, tall, thrall, trawl, wall, y'all, yawl. (2) appall, AWOL, baseball, befall, Bengal, cabal, catchall, COBOL, cure-all, curveball, enthrall, football, foosball, footfall, forestall, install, petrol, rainfall, recall, shortfall, snowfall, windfall. (3) aerosol, alcohol, bacchanal, basketball, cannonball, caterwaul, ethanol, folderol, free-for-all, gasohol, overhaul, parasol, protocol, vitriol, volleyball, waterfall, wherewithal. (4) cholesterol, Neanderthal.

-awld

(1) bald, scald. (2) piebald, so-called. (3) Archibald.
ALSO: -awl + -ed (i.e., crawled, enthralled).

-awlt

(1) alt, fault, halt, malt, salt, vault. (2) asphalt, assault, basalt, cobalt, default, exalt. (3) somersault.

-awltz

(1) waltz.
ALSO: -awlt + -s (i.e., faults, somersaults).

-awn

(1) awn, brawn, dawn, drawn, faun, fawn, gone, pawn, prawn, sawn, Sean, spawn, yawn. (2) bygone, indrawn, withdrawn. (3) Wobegone.

-awnch

(1) haunch, launch, paunch, staunch.

-awng

(1) gong, long, prong, song, strong, thong, throng, tong, wrong.
(2) along, belong, ding dong, diphthong, headlong, headstrong, Hong Kong, King Kong, lifelong, mahjong, oblong, ping-pong, prolong, sidelong. (3) evensong, overlong, Vietcong.

–awnk

(1) bonk, conch, conk, honk. (3) honky-tonk.

–awnt

(1) aunt, daunt, flaunt, gaunt, haunt, jaunt, taunt, vaunt, want.

–aws

(1) boss, cross, dross, floss, fosse, gloss, joss, loss, moss, Ross, sauce, toss. (2) across, lacrosse. (3) albatross, applesauce. (4) rhinoceros.

–awst

(1) cost, frost, lost. (2) accost, exhaust. (3) holocaust, Pentecost, permafrost.
ALSO: **–aws** + -*ed* (i.e., *crossed, tossed*)

–awt

(1) aught, bought, brought, caught, fought, fraught, naught, ought, sought, taught, taut, thought, wrought. (2) besought, distraught, dreadnought, forethought, onslaught. (3) aeronaut, afterthought, Argonaut, astronaut, cosmonaut, juggernaut, overwrought.

–awth

(1) broth, cloth, froth, moth, sloth, swath, troth, wroth. (2) betroth, broadcloth, sackcloth. (3) behemoth.

–awz

(1) cause, clause, gauze, hawse, pause. (2) applause, because.
(3) menopause, Santa Claus.
ALSO: **–aw** + -*s* (i.e., *flaws, macaws*).

–ay

(1) a, aye, bay, bey, brae, cay, clay, day, dray, Fay, fey, flay, fray, gay, gray, grey, hay, jay, Kay, lay, may, May, nay, née, neigh, pay, play, pray, prey, ray, say, shay, slay, sleigh, spay, splay, spray, stay, stray, sway, they, tray, trey, way, weigh, whey, yea. (2) affray, allay, array, assay, astray, away, aweigh, ballet, belay, beret, betray, Biscay, blue jay, Bombay, bouquet, Broadway, cadre, café, causeway, chambray, convey, crochet, decay, deejay, defray, delay, dismay, display, doomsday, endplay, essay, fillet, foray, foreplay, foyer, Friday, gainsay, gangway, halfway, hearsay, horseplay, hooray, inlay, inveigh, L.A., midday, midway, mislay, moiré, Monday, moray, naysay, nosegay, obey, olé, outstay, padre, passé, per se, pince-nez, portray, prepay, purée, purvey, Rabelais, relay, René, repay, replay, risqué,

roué, sachet, sashay, soirée, soufflé, subway, Sunday, survey, throughway, Thursday, today, touché, toupee, Tuesday, VJ, Wednesday, x-ray. (3) appliqué, Beaujolais, cabaret, canapé, cast-away, Chevrolet, consommé, disarray, disobey, DNA, émigré, exposé, faraway, fiancé(e), gamma ray, holiday, interplay, manta ray, matinee, Milky Way, Monterey, Namaste, negligee, overlay, overpay, overplay, overstay, popinjay, protégé(e), résumé, ricochet, roundelay, runaway, Saint-Tropez, San Jose, Santa Fe, Saturday, s'il vous plaît, sobriquet, stowaway, underlay, underpay, underplay, yesterday. (4) Appian Way, cabriolet, café au lait, communiqué, habitué, Olivier, papier maché. (5) cinema verité.

–ay-day

(2) heyday, May Day, payday, playday.

–oh-kay

(2) croquet, okay.

–ay-lay

(2) Malay, melee, waylay.

–ahn-tay

(2) Dante. (3) andante.

–ayb

(1) Abe, babe, nabe. (3) astrolabe.

–ayd

(1) aid, bade, blade, braid, cade, fade, glade, grade, jade, lade, laid, made, maid, paid, raid, rayed, shade, spade, staid, suede, they'd, trade, wade. (2) abrade, afraid, arcade, band-aid, blockade, brigade, brocade, cascade, charade, cockade, crusade, degrade, dissuade, evade, grenade, homemade, invade, limeade, mermaid, nightshade, orangeade, parade, persuade, pervade, pomade, post-paid, prepaid, self-made, stockade, tirade, unmade, unpaid, upbraid, waylaid, x-rayed. (3) accolade, Adelaide, ambuscade, balustrade, barricade, cannonade, cavalcade, centigrade, chambermaid, colonnade, custom-made, escalade, escapade, gallopade, lemonade, marinade, marmalade, masquerade, orangeade, overlaid, palisade, promenade, ready-made, renegade, retrograde, serenade, underpaid.
ALSO: –ay + -ed (i.e., *played*, *ricocheted*).

–ayf

(1) chafe, safe, strafe, waif. (2) fail-safe, unsafe, vouchsafe.

–ayj

(1) age, cage, gage, gauge, page, rage, sage, stage, swage, wage. (2) assuage, backstage, birdcage, Bronze Age, engage, enrage, front page, Ice Age, New Age, outrage, presage, space age, teenage. (3) disengage, Golden Age, Iron Age, overage, underage.

–ayk

(1) ache, bake, Blake, brake, break, cake, crake, drake, fake, flake, hake, Jake, lake, make, quake, rake, sake, shake, slake, snake, stake, steak, strake, take, wake. (2) awake, backache, bespake, betake, cornflake, daybreak, earache, earthquake, forsake, heartbreak, keepsake, mandrake, mistake, namesake, opaque, outbreak, partake, retake, snowflake, toothache. (3) bellyache, johnnycake, overtake, patty-cake, rattlesnake, stomachache, undertake, wedding cake.

–ayl

(1) ail, ale, bail, bale, Braille, dale, Dale, fail, flail, frail, Gael, Gail, gale, grail, hail, hale, jail, kale, mail, male, nail, pail, pale, quail, rail, sail, sale, scale, shale, snail, stale, swale, tail, tale, they'll, trail, vale, veil, wail, wale, whale, Yale. (2) assail, avail, bewail, bobtail, cocktail, curtail, detail, dovetail, entail, exhale, fantail, female, hobnail, impale, inhale, pigtail, prevail, regale, retail, travail, unveil, wholesale. (3) Abigail, countervail, farthingale, ginger ale, Holy Grail, martingale, monorail, nightingale, ponytail.

–aylz

(1) Wales.
ALSO: –ayl + -s (i.e., *ails*, *ales*)

–aym

(1) aim, blame, came, claim, dame, fame, flame, frame, game, lame, maim, name, same, shame, tame. (2) acclaim, aflame, became, beldame, declaim, defame, disclaim, exclaim, inflame, misname, nickname, proclaim, reclaim, surname. (3) overcame.

–ayn

(1) bane, blain, Blaine, brain, Cain, cane, chain, crane, Dane, deign, drain, fain, fane, feign, gain, grain, Jane, lain, lane, main, Maine, mane, pain, pane, plain, plane, rain, reign, rein, sane, seine, skein, slain, Spain, sprain, stain, strain, swain, thane, train, twain, vain, vane, vein, wain, wane, Zane. (2) abstain, again, airplane, arcane, arraign, attain, biplane, campaign, champagne, Champlain, chicane, chilblain, chow mein, cocaine, complain, constrain, contain, demesne, detain, dogbane, Duquesne, Elaine, enchain, entrain, ethane, explain, germane, henbane, humane, Hussein, inane, insane, Lorraine, maintain, membrane, methane, migraine, moraine, murrain, obtain, ordain, pertain, plantain, procaine, profane, quatrain, refrain, regain, remain, restrain, retain, Sinn Fein, sustain, terrain, Ukraine, urbane, wolfsbane. (3) aeroplane, appertain, ascertain, cellophane, Charlemagne, chatelaine, counterpane, entertain, frangipane, hurricane, hydroplane, Mary Jane, monoplane, scatterbrain, weather vane, windowpane. (4) legerdemain.

–oh-mayn

(2) domain, ptomaine, romaine.

–aynj

(1) change, grange, mange, range, strange. (2) arrange, derange, estrange, exchange. (3) disarrange, interchange, rearrange.

–aynt

(1) ain't, faint, feint, mayn't, paint, plaint, quaint, saint, taint.
(2) acquaint, attaint, complaint, constraint, Geraint, greasepaint, restraint.

–ayp

(1) ape, cape, chape, crepe, drape, grape, jape, nape, rape, scrape, shape, tape. (2) agape, escape, landscape, moonscape, seascape, shipshape, undrape. (3) audiotape, videotape.

–ayps

(1) traipse. (3) jackanapes.
ALSO: –ayp + -s (i.e., *apes*, *escapes*).

–ays

(1) ace, base, bass, brace, case, chase, dace, face, grace, Grace, lace, mace, pace, place, plaice, race, space, Thrace, trace, vase. (2) abase, apace, birthplace, briefcase, debase, disgrace, displace, efface, embrace, encase, erase, grimace, horserace, misplace, outface, outpace, rat race, reface, replace, retrace, staircase, ukase, uncase, unlace. (3) about-face, aerospace, carapace, commonplace, contrabass, funny face, interlace, interspace, marketplace, outer space, pillowcase, steeplechase.

–ayst

(1) baste, chaste, haste, paste, taste, waist, waste. (2) distaste, foretaste, unchaste. (3) aftertaste.
ALSO: –ays + -ed (i.e., *aced, refaced*).

–ayt

(1) ait, ate, bait, bate, crate, date, eight, fate, fête, freight, gait, gate, grate, great, hate, Kate, late, mate, Nate, pate, plait, plate, prate, rate, sate, skate, slate, spate, state, straight, strait, Tate, trait, wait, weight. (2) abate, aerate, agnate, await, berate, bookplate, casemate, castrate, caudate, cellmate, cerate, checkmate, chlorate, chromate, citrate, classmate, cognate, collate, comate, conflate, connate, create, cremate, crenate, crispate, curate, debate, deflate, dentate, dictate, dilate, donate, elate, equate, estate, falcate, filtrate, flyweight, frustrate, gradate, hastate, helpmate, hotplate, hydrate, ice skate, inflate, ingrate, inmate, innate, instate, jailbait, jugate, Kuwait, lactate, legate, lichgate, ligate, lightweight, locate, lunate, lustrate, magnate, mandate, messmate, migrate, misdate, misstate, mutate, narrate, negate, nitrate, notate, oblate, orate, ornate, ovate, palmate, palpate, phonate, phosphate, pinnate, placate, playmate, prelate, primate, prorate, prostate, prostrate, pulsate, quadrate, rebate, relate, restate, rotate, sedate, serrate, shipmate, soulmate, stagnate, stalemate, striate, sublate, sulfate, template, ternate, testate, translate, truncate, vacate, vibrate, Vulgate. (3) abdicate, abnegate, abrogate, acclimate, acetate, adequate, adulate, adumbrate, advocate, aggravate, agitate, allocate, altercate, ambulate, amputate, animate, annotate, antedate, antiquate, apostate, approbate, arbitrate, arrogate, aspirate, aureate, aviate, bifurcate, branchiate, cachinnate, calculate, calibrate, caliphate, candidate, captivate, carbonate, castigate, celebrate, ciliate, circulate, cogitate, colligate, collimate, collocate, compensate, complicate, concentrate, confiscate, congregate, conjugate, consecrate, constipate, consummate, contemplate, copulate, correlate, corrugate, coruscate, crenellate, crepitate, culminate, cultivate, cumulate, cuspidate, decimate, defalcate, def-

ecate, dehydrate, delegate, demarcate, demonstrate, denigrate, denudate, depilate, deprecate, depredate, derogate, desecrate, desiccate, designate, detonate, devastate, deviate, dislocate, dissipate, distillate, divagate, dominate, duplicate, educate, elevate, elongate, emanate, emigrate, emulate, enervate, estimate, excavate, exculpate, execrate, expiate, explicate, extirpate, extricate, fabricate, fascinate, featherweight, fecundate, fenestrate, fibrillate, flagellate, fluctuate, foliate, formicate, formulate, fornicate, fulgurate, fulminate, fumigate, geminate, generate, germinate, glaciate, gladiate, Golden Gate, graduate, granulate, gravitate, heavyweight, hebetate, hesitate, hibernate, hyphenate, ideate, illustrate, imbricate, imitate, immigrate, immolate, implicate, imprecate, impregnate, incarnate, incubate, inculcate, inculpate, indicate, indurate, infiltrate, innervate, innovate, insensate, instigate, insufflate, insulate, integrate, interstate, intimate, intonate, inundate, irrigate, irritate, isolate, iterate, jubilate, lacerate, laminate, legislate, levitate, liberate, lineate, liquidate, litigate, lubricate, macerate, machinate, magistrate, masticate, mediate, medicate, meditate, menstruate, militate, mitigate, moderate, modulate, motivate, mutilate, nauseate, navigate, nominate, nucleate, obfuscate, obligate, obviate, operate, orchestrate, ordinate, oscillate, overweight, ovulate, paginate, palliate, palpitate, paperweight, penetrate, percolate, perforate, permeate, perpetrate, pollinate, populate, postulate, potentate, predicate, procreate, promulgate, propagate, proximate, punctuate, radiate, recreate, regulate, reinstate, relegate, remonstrate, renovate, replicate, reprobate, resonate, roseate, rubricate, ruminate, rusticate, salivate, sanitate, satiate, saturate, scintillate, segregate, separate, seriate, sibilate, silicate, simulate, sinuate, situate, speculate, staminate, stimulate, stipulate, strangulate, subjugate, sublimate, suffocate, supplicate, syncopate, syndicate, tabulate, terminate, titillate, tolerate, transmigrate, triplicate, ulcerate, ululate, undulate, underrate, understate, underweight, ungulate, urinate, vaccinate, vacillate, validate, vegetate, venerate, ventilate, vertebrate, vindicate, violate, vitiate, Watergate, welterweight.
(4) abbreviate, abominate, accelerate, accentuate, accommodate, accumulate, acuminate, adjudicate, adulterate, affiliate, agglomerate, alienate, alleviate, amalgamate, annihilate, annunciate, anticipate, apostolate, appreciate, appropriate, approximate, articulate, asphyxiate, assassinate, asseverate, assimilate, associate, attenuate, authenticate, calumniate, capitulate, coagulate, commemorate, commiserate, communicate, concatenate, conciliate, congratulate, consolidate, contaminate, cooperate, coordinate, corroborate, debilitate, decapitate, degenerate, deliberate, delineate, denunciate, depopulate, depreciate, dilapidate,

discriminate, disseminate, dissimulate, dissociate, domesticate, effectuate, ejaculate, elaborate, electroplate, eliminate, elucidate, emaciate, emancipate, emasculate, enumerate, enunciate, equilibrate, equivocate, eradiate, eradicate, evacuate, evaluate, evaporate, eventuate, eviscerate, exacerbate, exaggerate, exasperate, excogitate, excoriate, excruciate, exfoliate, exhilarate, exonerate, expatiate, expatriate, expectorate, expostulate, expropriate, extenuate, exterminate, extrapolate, extravagate, exuberate, facilitate, felicitate, gesticulate, habilitate, habituate, hallucinate, humiliate, hydrogenate, hypothecate, illuminate, impersonate, impropriate, inaugurate, incarcerate, incinerate, incorporate, incriminate, indoctrinate, inebriate, infatuate, infuriate, ingratiate, initiate, inoculate, inordinate, insatiate, inseminate, insinuate, inspectorate, interrogate, intimidate, intoxicate, invalidate, invertebrate, investigate, invigorate, inviolate, irradiate, itinerate, legitimate, luxuriate, manipulate, meliorate, miscalculate, necessitate, negotiate, obliterate, officiate, orientate, originate, participate, particulate, peregrinate, perpetuate, pontificate, precipitate, predominate, procrastinate, proliferate, propitiate, quadruplicate, reanimate, reciprocate, recriminate, recuperate, redecorate, reduplicate, refrigerate, regenerate, regurgitate, reiterate, rejuvenate, repopulate, repudiate, resuscitate, retaliate, reticulate, reverberate, somnambulate, sophisticate, subordinate, substantiate, transliterate, triangulate, trifoliate, variegate, vicariate, vituperate, vociferate. (5) ameliorate, circumambulate, circumnavigate, circumstantiate, deteriorate, differentiate, discombobulate, excommunicate, incapacitate, misappropriate, recapitulate, rehabilitate, reinvigorate.

–oh-bayt

(2) globate, probate.

–uhr-gayt

(3) expurgate, objurgate.

–ee-layt

(3) constellate. (4) interpellate, interpolate.

–ei-rayt

(2) gyrate, irate, lyrate.

–aythh

(1) eighth, faith, Faith, wraith. (3) interfaith.

–ayth

(1) bathe, lathe, scathe, swathe.

–ayv

(1) brave, cave, crave, Dave, gave, glaive, grave, knave, lave, nave, pave, rave, save, shave, slave, stave, they've, waive, wave. (2) behave, concave, conclave, deprave, enclave, engrave, enslave, exclave, forgave, margrave. (3) architrave, microwave.

–ayz

(1) baize, blaze, braise, braze, chaise, craze, daze, faze, gaze, glaze, graze, haze, maize, maze, phase, phrase, praise, raise, raze. (2) ablaze, amaze, appraise, catchphrase, dispraise, liaise, malaise, stargaze. (3) mayonnaise, nowadays, paraphrase, polonaise.
ALSO: **–ay** + -*s* (i.e., *bays*, *surveys*).

–ee

(1) be, Bea, bee, Brie, Cree, fee, flea, flee, free, gee, glee, he, key, knee, lea, lee, Leigh, me, pea, pee, plea, sea, see, she, ski, spree, tea, thee, three, tree, we, wee, ye. (2) acme, agree, Billy, CD, debris, decree, degree, ennui, foresee, goatee, grandee, grantee, harpy, lessee, levee, marquee, marquis, murky, rupee, settee, silly, spondee, trochee, trophy, trustee, wacky. (3) ABC, absentee, adobe, addressee, agony, anomie, amputee, apogee, assignee, baloney, botany, bourgeoisie, bumblebee, calorie, calumny, canopy, Cherokee, chickadee, chimpanzee, C.O.D., company, coterie, DDT, debauchee, destiny, devotee, disagree, ebony, energy, felony, filigree, fleur-de-lis, fricassee, gluttony, guarantee, harmony, irony, jamboree, licensee, maître d', manatee, Mercury, mutiny, nominee, Normandy, pedigree, perigee, Pharisee, potpourri, prophecy, Ptolemy, recipe, referee, refugee, repartee, sesame, simile, simony, symphony, synergy, tyranny, VIP, vis-à-vis, wannabe, warranty, willowy. (4) abalone, anemone, anomaly, apostrophe, Antigone, astronomy, biology, caller ID, calliope, catastrophe, chemistry, facsimile, geography, geometry, Gethsemane, hokey-pokey, hyperbole, Karaoke, macaroni, melancholy, philosophy, proclivity, synonymy. (5) aborigine, biochemistry, Deuteronomy, sociology, trigonometry.
ALSO: Words created by addition of suffix -*y* (i.e., *trusty*, *summery*).

–ahr-ee

(2) sari, starry. (3) hari-kari, Mata Hari.

–ehr-ee

(2) aerie, airy, Barry, berry, bury, Carrie, carry, chary, cherry, dairy, Derry, fairy, ferry, Gary, hairy, Harry, Jerry, Kerry, Larry, marry, Mary, merry, nary, parry, Perry, prairie, scary, sherry, Sherry, tarry, Terry, vary, very, wary. (3) blackberry, blueberry, canary, contrary, cranberry, gooseberry, miscarry, mulberry, raspberry, strawberry, unwary, vagary. (4) actuary, adversary, ancillary, antiquary, arbitrary, beriberi, boysenberry, capillary, cassowary, cautionary, cemetery, centenary, commentary, commissary, corollary, culinary, customary, dictionary, dietary, dignitary, dromedary, elderberry, estuary, February, formulary, functionary, hari-kari, honorary, huckleberry, intermarry, Janissary, January, lamasery, legendary, legionary, literary, loganberry, luminary, mercenary, military, millinery, momentary, monastery, monetary, mortuary, necessary, ordinary, planetary, presbytery, pulmonary, reliquary, salivary, salutary, sanctuary, sanguinary, sanitary, secondary, secretary, sedentary, seminary, solitary, stationary, stationery, statuary, sublunary, sumptuary, temporary, tertiary, tributary, tutelary, visionary, voluntary, vulnerary. (5) ablutionary, apothecary, confectionary, constabulary, contemporary, depositary, epistolary, fiduciary, hereditary, imaginary, incendiary, involuntary, obituary, pecuniary, proprietary, residuary, vocabulary, voluptuary. (6) beneficiary, evolutionary, extraordinary, intermediary, revolutionary.

–ing-ee

(2) clingy, dinghy, springy, stringy, swingy, zingy.

–ink-ee

(2) dinky, inky, kinky, pinky. (3) Helsinki.

–ir-ee

(2) aerie, beery, bleary, cheery, dearie, dreary, eerie, Erie, leery, query, smeary, weary. (3) Lake Erie, road-weary, world-weary.
(4) miserere.

–oh-ee

(2) blowy, Bowie, Chloe, doughy, Joey, showy, snowy, Zoe.

–ohr-ee

(2) Dorie, dory, glory, gory, hoary, Laurie, lorry, quarry, sorry, storey, story, Tory. (3) Old Glory, vainglory. (4) allegory, a priori, category, desultory, dilatory, dormitory, gustatory, hortatory, hunky-dory,

inventory, laudatory, mandatory, migratory, offertory, oratory, peremptory, predatory, prefatory, promissory, promontory, purgatory, repertory, territory. (5) adulatory, a fortiori, cacciatore, circulatory, commendatory, compensatory, conciliatory, conservatory, declaratory, defamatory, depilatory, depository, deprecatory, derogatory, exclamatory, explanatory, inflammatory, laboratory, obligatory, observatory, preparatory, reformatory, respiratory, undulatory. (6) a posteriori, retaliatory.

–oo-ee

(2) buoy, chewy, dewy, fluey, gluey, gooey, hooey, Louie, Louis, phooey, screwy. (3) chop suey. (4) ratatouille.

–owr-ee

(2) bowery, cowry, dowry, flowery, Maori, showery.

–uhr-ee

(2) burry, curry, flurry, furry, fury, houri, hurry, jury, scurry, slurry, surrey, worry. (3) Missouri, tandoori.

–aa-bee

(2) abbey, Abby, cabby, crabby, flabby, Gaby, grabby, scabby, shabby, tabby.

–ah-bee

(2) bobby, Bobby, cobby, hobby, knobby, lobby, Robby, snobby.

–ahm-bee

(2) zombie. (4) Abercrombie.

–ay-bee

(2) baby, maybe.

–oh-bee

(2) obi, Gobi, Toby. (3) adobe, Nairobi.

–oo-bee

(2) booby, ruby, Ruby.

–uh-bee

(2) chubby, cubby, grubby, hubby, knubby, scrubby, shrubby, stubby, tubby.

–ah-chee

(2) blotchy, bocce, botchy, splotchy. (3) huarache, vivace.
(4) Liberace.

–ee-chee

(2) lichee, litchi, Nietzsche, peachy, preachy, screechy.

–i-chee

(2) bitchy, itchy, pitchy, twitchy.

–aa-dee

(2) caddy, daddy, faddy, laddie, paddy. (4) finnan haddie, sugar daddy.

–aan-dee

(2) Andy, bandy, brandy, candy, dandy, handy, Mandy, pandy, randy, Randy, sandy, Sandy. (3) jim-dandy, unhandy.

–ah-dee

(2) body, cloddy, Mahdi, noddy, Roddy, shoddy, Soddy, toddy, wadi. (3) embody, nobody, somebody. (4) anybody, busybody, everybody.

–ahr-dee

(2) hardy, lardy, tardy. (3) foolhardy.

–aw-dee

(2) bawdy, gaudy.

–awl-dee

(2) Grimaldi, Vivaldi. (3) Garibaldi.

–ay-dee

(2) lady, Sadie, shady. (3) landlady.

–ee-dee

(2) beady, greedy, needy, reedy, seedy, speedy, tweedy, weedy.

–eh-dee

(2) eddy, Eddie, Freddy, heady, ready, steady, Teddy. (3) already, unready, unsteady.

–i-dee

(2) biddy, giddy, kiddy, middy, midi.

–in-dee

(2) Hindi, lindy, shindy, windy.

–oo-dee

(2) broody, Judy, moody, Trudy.

–ow-dee

(2) cloudy, dowdy, howdy, rowdy. (3) pandowdy.

–uh-dee

(2) bloody, buddy, cruddy, muddy, ruddy, study. (4) fuddy-duddy, understudy.

–uhn-dee

(2) Monday, Sunday, undie. (4) jaguarundi, salmagundi.
(5) coatimundi.

–uhr-dee

(2) birdie, sturdy, wordy. (4) hurdy-gurdy.

–uu-dee (–uu-tee)

(2) goody, sooty, woody.

–aa-fee

(2) chaffy, daffy, draffy, taffy.

–ah-fee (–aw-fee)

(2) coffee, toffee.

–ee-fee

(2) beefy, leafy.

–i-fee

(2) iffy, jiffy, spiffy.

–oh-fee

(2) Sophie, strophe, trophy.

–uh-fee

(2) fluffy, huffy, puffy, scruffy, stuffy. (4) orange roughy.

–aa-gee

(2) Aggie, baggy, craggy, Maggie, scraggy, shaggy.

–ah-gee

(2) boggy, cloggy, doggy, foggy, groggy, soggy.

–eh-gee

(2) dreggy, leggy, Peggy.

–oh-gee

(2) bogey, bogie, doggie, fogy, stogie, Yogi.

–uh-gee

(2) buggy, muggy.

–ing-glee

(2) jingly, shingly, singly, tingly.

–ayn-jee

(2) mangy, rangy.

–in-jee

(2) dingy, fringy, stingy.

–uhd-jee

(2) pudgy, smudgy.

–uhr-jee

(2) clergy. (3) liturgy. (4) dramaturgy, metallurgy, thaumaturgy.

–aa-kee

(2) Jackie, khaki, lackey, tacky, wacky.

–ah-kee

(2) cocky, flocky, hockey, jockey, rocky, sake, saki, schlocky, stocky. (3) Iraqi. (4) Jabberwocky, Kawasaki, Nagasaki, sukiyaki, teriyaki.

–ahr-kee

(2) barky, darky, marquee, sparky. (3) anarchy, malarkey, monarchy. (4) hierarchy, matriarchy, oligarchy, patriarchy.

–i-kee

(2) dickey, Dicky, Mickey, Nicky, quickie, rickey, Ricky, sticky, tricky, Vicky.

–il-kee

(2) milky, silky.

–is-kee

(2) frisky, risky, whisky.

–oh-kee

(2) choky, croaky, hokey, poky, smoky, troche, trochee. (4) hokey-pokey, karaoke, okey-dokey.

–oo-kee

(2) fluky, kooky, spooky. (3) Kabuki.

–uh-kee

(2) ducky, lucky, mucky, plucky. (3) Kentucky, unlucky.

–uhl-kee

(2) bulky, hulky, sulky.

–uhng-kee

(2) chunky, donkey, flunky, funky, hunky, junky, monkey, spunky.

–uhr-kee

(2) jerky, murky, perky, turkey, Turkey.

–uhs-kee

(2) dusky, husky, muskie, musky.

–uu-kee

(2) bookie, cookie, hooky, nooky, rookie.

–aa-lee

(2) alley, bally, challis, dally, galley, pally, rally, sally, Sally, tally, valley. (3) bialy, Death Valley, finale. (4) dillydally, shilly-shally.

–aad-lee

(2) badly, gladly, madly, sadly.

–aank-lee

(2) blankly, dankly, frankly, lankly, rankly.

–aast-lee

(2) ghastly, lastly, vastly.

–aakt-**lee**

(3) abstractly, compactly, exactly.

–ah-**lee**

(2) Bali, collie, dolly, Dolly, folly, golly, holly, jolly, Molly, Polly, trolley, volley. (3) finale, loblolly, tamale. (4) melancholy.

–ahd-**lee**

(2) godly, oddly. (3) ungodly.

–ahng-**lee** (–awng-**lee**)

(2) strongly, wrongly.

–ahr-**lee**

(2) barley, Charlie, gnarly, parley, snarly.

–ahrk-**lee**

(2) darkly, sparkly, starkly.

–ahrt-**lee**

(2) partly, smartly, tartly.

–aht-**lee**

(2) hotly, motley.

–ay-**lee**

(2) bailey, Bailey, daily, gaily, Haley, palely, scaly. (3) Disraeli, Israeli, shillelagh. (4) motte and bailey, ukulele

–aym-**lee**

(2) gamely, lamely, namely, tamely.

–ayn-**lee**

(2) mainly, plainly, sanely, vainly. (3) humanely, inanely, insanely, mundanely, profanely, ungainly, urbanely.

–ayv-**lee**

(2) bravely, gravely.

–ee-**lee**

(2) eely, freely, mealy, really, steely. (3) genteelly, surreally, Swahili. (4) campanili, touchy-feely.

–eef-lee

(2) briefly, chiefly.

–eek-lee

(2) bleakly, meekly, sleekly, treacly, weakly, weekly. (3) biweekly, obliquely, uniquely. (4) semiweekly.

–eem-lee

(2) seemly. (3) extremely, supremely, unseemly.

–een-lee

(2) cleanly, keenly, leanly, meanly, queenly. (3) obscenely, routinely, serenely.

–eep-lee

(2) cheaply, deeply, steeply.

–eest-lee

(2) beastly, priestly.

–eet-lee

(2) fleetly, neatly, sweetly. (3) completely, discreetly, discretely. (4) incompletely, indiscreetly.

–eh-lee

(2) belly, Delhi, deli, felly, jelly, Kelly, Nelly, Shelley, shelly, smelly, telly. (3) potbelly, rakehelly, New Delhi. (4) Botticelli, vermicelli. (5) Machiavelli.

–ehd-lee

(2) deadly, medley.

–ehkt-lee

(3) abjectly, correctly, directly, erectly. (4) incorrectly, indirectly.

–ehmb-lee

(2) trembly. (3) assembly.

–ehr-lee

(2) barely, fairly, rarely, squarely, yarely. (3) unfairly. (4) debonairly.

–ei-lee

(2) dryly, highly, Riley, shyly, slyly, smiley, wily, wryly.

–eid-lee

(2) idly, widely.

–eild-lee

(2) mildly, wildly.

–eim-lee

(2) primely, timely. (3) sublimely, untimely.

–ein-lee

(2) finely. (3) benignly, divinely, supinely.

–eind-lee

(2) blindly, kindly. (3) unkindly.

–eir-lee

(2) direly. (3) entirely.

–eis-lee

(2) nicely. (3) concisely, precisely.

–eit-lee

(2) brightly, knightly, lightly, nightly, sprightly, tightly, tritely.
(3) politely, unsightly. (4) impolitely.

–i-lee

(2) billy, Billy, Chile, chili, chilly, filly, frilly, gillie, hilly, lily, Lily,
Millie, shrilly, silly, stilly, Tillie, Willie. (3) bacilli, daylily, fusilli.
(4) Piccadilly, piccalilli, tiger lily, water lily, willy-nilly.

–ik-lee

(2) prickly, quickly, sickly, slickly, thickly.

–im-lee

(2) dimly, grimly, primly, trimly.

–imp-lee

(2) dimply, limply, pimply, simply.

–in-lee

(2) inly, thinly.

–inkt-lee

(3) distinctly, succinctly. (4) indistinctly.

–ir-lee

(2) clearly, dearly, merely, nearly, queerly, yearly. (3) austerely, severely, sincerely. (4) cavalierly, insincerely.

–iz-lee

(2) drizzly, grisly, grizzly.

–oh-lee

(2) drolly, goalie, holy, lowly, moly, slowly, solely, wholly. (3) aioli, cannoli, frijole. (4) guacamole, holy-moly, ravioli, roly-poly.

–ohn-lee

(2) lonely, only.

–ohrs-lee

(2) coarsely, hoarsely.

–ohrt-lee

(2) courtly, portly.

–ohs-lee

(2) closely, grossly. (3) jocosely, morosely, verbosely.

–ohst-lee

(2) ghostly, mostly.

–oo-lee

(2) coolie, coolly, coulee, duly, Julie, newly, stoolie, truly.
(3) patchouli, tabbouleh, unduly, unruly.

–ood-lee

(2) crudely, lewdly, rudely, shrewdly.

–ownd-lee

(2) roundly, soundly. (3) profoundly, unsoundly.

–owr-lee

(2) hourly, sourly.

–oy-lee

(2) coyly, doily, oily, roily.

–uh-lee

(2) cully, dully, gully, sully.

–uhb-lee

(2) bubbly, doubly, nubbly, stubbly.

–uhf-lee

(2) bluffly, gruffly, roughly, toughly.

–uhg-lee

(2) smugly, snuggly, ugly.

–uhm-lee

(2) comely, dumbly, numbly.

–uhr-lee

(2) burly, curly, early, girlie, hurly, knurly, pearly, purely, Shirley, squirrelly, surely, surly, swirly, whirly. (3) demurely, maturely, obscurely, securely. (4) hurly-burly.

–uhrd-lee

(2) thirdly. (3) absurdly.

–uhrt-lee

(2) curtly, pertly. (3) alertly, expertly, inertly, overtly. (4) inexpertly.

–uhst-lee

(2) justly. (3) augustly, robustly, unjustly.

–uu-lee

(2) bully, fully, pulley, wooly.

–aa-mee

(2) chamois, clammy, gammy, Grammy, hammy, mammy, Sammy, Tammy, whammy. (3) Miami.

–ah-mee

(2) swami, Tommy. (3) pastrami, salami, tsunami. (4) origami.

–ahr-mee

(2) army, barmy.

–ei-mee

(2) blimey, grimy, limey, limy, rimy, slimy, stymie, thymy.

–i-mee

(2) gimme, jimmy, Jimmy, shimmy, Timmy.

–oo-mee

(2) bloomy, gloomy, plumy, rheumy, roomy.

–uh-mee

(2) crumby, crummy, dummy, gummy, mummy, plumy, rummy, scummy, slummy, tummy, yummy.

–uhr-mee

(2) fermi, germy, squirmy, wormy. (3) diathermy, taxidermy.

–aa-nee

(2) Annie, canny, cranny, Danny, fanny, Fanny, granny, Manny, nanny. (3) uncanny. (4) frangipani, hootenanny.

–aak-nee

(2) acne, hackney.

–ah-nee

(2) Bonnie, bonny, Connie, Donny, Johnny, Lonny, nonny, Ronnie, Yanni.

–aw-nee

(2) brawny, lawny, Pawnee, scrawny, Shawnee, tawny.

–ay-nee

(2) brainy, grainy, rainy, zany. (4) Allegheny, miscellany.

–ee-nee

(2) beanie, genie, meanie, queenie, teeny, weenie. (3) bikini, Houdini, linguine, martini, Puccini, zucchini. (4) fettuccine, Mussolini, scaloppini, Tetrazzini, tortellini.

–eh-nee

(2) any, Benny, Denny, fenny, jenny, Jenny, Kenny, Lenny, many, penny, Penny.

–ei-nee

(2) briny, piney, shiny, spiny, tiny, twiny, viny, whiney, winy. (3) sunshiny.

–i-nee

(2) finny, guinea, Guinea, hinny, mini, Minnie, ninny, pinny, Pliny, skinny, spinney, tinny, Vinnie, whinny, Winnie. (4) ignominy.

–id-nee

(2) kidney, Sidney, Sydney.

–oh-nee

(2) bony, Coney, crony, Mony, phony, pony, stony, Toni, tony, Tony. (3) baloney, Marconi, Shoshone, spumoni, tortoni. (4) abalone, alimony, antimony, cannelloni, ceremony, ciceroni, macaroni, matrimony, minestrone, palimony, rigatoni, parsimony, patrimony, sanctimony, testimony, zabaglione. (5) phony baloney.

–ohr-nee

(2) corny, horny, thorny.

–oo-nee

(2) goony, loony, moony.

–ow-nee

(2) brownie, Brownie, downy, towny.

–uh-nee

(2) bunny, funny, gunny, honey, money, sonny, sunny, tunny.

–uhr-nee

(2) Bernie, Ernie, gurney, journey, tourney. (3) attorney.

–aa-pee

(2) happy, nappy, sappy, scrappy, snappy. (3) slap-happy, unhappy.

–ah-pee

(2) choppy, copy, croppy, floppy, poppy, sloppy, soppy. (3) jalopy, serape. (4) photocopy.

–ee-pee

(2) creepy, sleepy, tepee, weepy.

–i-pee

(2) dippy, drippy, hippy, lippy, nippy, snippy, tippy, trippy, zippy. (4) Mississippi.

–is-pee

(2) crispy, wispy.

–oh-pee

(2) dopey, Hopi, mopey, ropy, soapy, topi.

–oo-pee

(2) croupy, droopy, groupie, poopy, rupee, soupy, whoopee.

–uh-pee

(2) guppy, puppy, yuppie.

–awd-ree

(2) Audrey, bawdry, tawdry.

–ei-ree

(2) briery, diary, fiery, friary, miry, priory, spiry, wiry. (3) enquiry, inquiry.

–aa-see

(2) brassy, chassis, classy, gassy, glassy, grassy, lassie, massy, sassy.
(4) Malagasy, Tallahassee.

–aak-see

(2) taxi, waxy. (4) galaxy.

–aan-see

(2) chancy, Clancy, fancy, Nancy. (4) chiromancy, geomancy, hydromancy, lithomancy, militancy, necromancy, sycophancy.
(5) bibliomancy, botanomancy, crystallomancy.

–ah-see (–aw-see)

(2) bossy, drossy, Flossie, flossy, glossy, mossy, posse, quasi.

–ahk-see

(2) doxy, foxy, moxie, proxy. (3) Biloxi. (4) orthodoxy.
(5) heterodoxy, unorthodoxy.

–ahp-see

(2) dropsy. (3) autopsy, biopsy.

–ay-see

(2) Casey, lacy, Macy, racy.

–ee-see

(2) creasy, fleecy, greasy, specie.

–eh-see

(2) Bessie, dressy, Jesse, messy, Tessie.

–ehk-see

(2) prexy, sexy. (3) apoplexy.

–ehp-see

(2) Pepsi. (4) catalepsy, epilepsy.

–ei-see

(2) icy, pricey, spicy.

–ik-see

(2) Dixie, nixie, pixie.

–ip-see

(2) gypsy, ipse, tipsy. (3) Poughkeepsie.

–oo-see

(2) goosy, juicy, Lucy, sluicy. (3) Watusi.

–ow-see

(2) blousy, mousy.

–uh-see

(2) fussy, gussy, hussy, mussy.

–aa-shee

(2) ashy, flashy, mashie, splashy, trashy.

–ah-shee

(2) sloshy, squashy, washy.

–uh-shee

(2) gushy, mushy, plushy, slushy.

–ahr-slee

(2) parsley, sparsely.

–ay-stee

(2) hasty, pasty, tasty.

–aa-tee

(2) batty, chatty, fatty, gnatty, Hattie, Mattie, natty, patty, Patty, ratty. (4) Cincinnati.

–aaf-tee

(2) crafty, drafty.

–aan-tee

(2) ante, anti, auntie, scanty, shanty. (3) Bacchante, Chianti, infante.
(4) vigilante.

–ah-tee

(2) blotty, clotty, Dottie, dotty, knotty, Lottie, potty, snotty, spotty.
(3) basmati, karate. (4) digerati, glitterati, literati.

–ahf-tee (–awf-tee)

(2) lofty, softy.

–ahn-tee

(2) Dante. (3) Bacchante, andante, Chianti, infante. (4) dilettante.

–ahr-tee

(2) Arte, hearty, party, smarty. (3) ex parte, Havarti.

–aw-tee

(2) haughty, naughty.

–awl-tee

(2) faulty, salty.

–ay-tee

(2) eighty, Haiti, Katie, matey, platy, weighty.

–ee-tee

(2) meaty, peaty, sleety, sweetie, treaty, ziti. (3) entreaty, Tahiti.

–eh-tee

(2) Betty, Hetty, jetty, Lettie, Nettie, petit, petty, sweaty.
(3) confetti, libretti, machete, spaghetti. (4) spermaceti.

–ehn-tee

(2) plenty, twenty, sente. (3) al dente, aplenty, licente.
(4) twenty-twenty.

–ehs-tee

(2) chesty, testy, zesty.

–ei-tee

(2) flighty, mighty, nightie, whitey. (3) almighty. (4) Aphrodite.

–i-tee

(2) city, ditty, gritty, kitty, Kitty, pity, pretty, witty. (3) banditti, committee. (4) nitty-gritty, Salt Lake City, subcommittee.

–if-tee

(2) drifty, fifty, nifty, shifty, thrifty.

–in-tee

(2) flinty, linty, minty, squinty.

–oh-tee

(2) dhoti, goatee, throaty, zloty. (3) chayote, coyote, peyote.
(4) Don Quixote.

–ohr-tee

(2) forty, sortie, sporty, warty.

–oo-tee

(2) beauty, booty, cootie, cutie, duty, fluty, fruity, snooty. (3) agouti.
(4) tutti-frutti.

–own-tee

(2) bounty, county, mounty.

–ow-tee

(2) doughty, droughty, gouty, pouty.

–oyl-tee

(2) loyalty, royalty.

–uh-tee

(2) nutty, puttee, putty, rutty, smutty.

–uhr-tee

(2) cherty, dirty, flirty, Gertie, thirty.

–uhs-tee

(2) busty, crusty, dusty, gusty, lusty, musty, rusty, trusty.

–i-thhee

(2) pithy, smithy.

–aan-**tree**
(2) chantry, gantry, pantry.

–ehn-**tree**
(2) entry, gentry, sentry.

–in-**tree**
(2) splintery, wintry.

–uhl-**tree**
(2) sultry. (3) adultery.

–ay-**vee**
(2) cavy, Davy, gravy, navy, wavy.

–eh-**vee**
(2) bevy, Chevy, heavy, levee, levy. (3) top-heavy.

–i-**vee**
(2) civie, divvy, privy, skivvy. (3) tantivy.

–uhr-**vee**
(2) curvy, nervy, scurvy. (4) topsy-turvy.

–aan-**zee**
(2) pansy, tansy.

–ay-**zee**
(2) crazy, daisy, hazy, lazy, mazy. (3) stir-crazy. (4) oops-a-daisy.

–ee-**zee**
(2) breezy, cheesy, easy, queasy, sleazy, sneezy, wheezy.
(3) Parcheesi, speakeasy, uneasy.

–i-**zee**
(2) busy, dizzy, frizzy, Lizzie, tizzy.

–im-**zee**
(2) flimsy, whimsy.

–oh-**zee**
(2) cozy, dozy, nosy, posy, prosy, Rosie, rosy.

–oo-zee

(2) boozy, floozy, newsy, oozy, Uzi, woozy.

–ow-zee

(2) blousy, drowsy, frowsy, lousy.

–uh-zee

(2) fuzzy, muzzy, skuzzy. (4) fuzzy-wuzzy.

–uhr-zee

(2) furzy, jersey, Jersey, kersey.

–eech

(1) beach, beech, bleach, breach, breech, each, leach, leech, peach, preach, reach, screech, teach. (2) beseech, impeach. (3) overreach, out-of-reach.

–eed

(1) bead, bleed, breed, cede, creed, deed, feed, greed, heed, knead, lead, mead, Mede, meed, need, plead, read, reed, seed, screed, skied, speed, steed, Swede, tweed, weed. (2) Candide, concede, exceed, Godspeed, impede, indeed, misdeed, mislead, precede, proceed, recede, secede, stampede, succeed. (3) aniseed, centipede, Ganymede, ironweed, millipede, overfeed, supersede. (4) velocipede.
ALSO: **–ee** + *-ed* (i.e., *freed*, *agreed*).

–ehr-eed

(2) carried, harried, married, parried, tarried, varied. (3) miscarried, remarried, unmarried, unvaried. (4) intermarried.

–aan-deed

(2) bandied, brandied, candied.

–eef

(1) beef, brief, chief, fief, grief, leaf, reef, sheaf, thief. (2) belief, fig leaf, relief. (3) bas-relief, cloverleaf, disbelief, handkerchief, interleaf, leitmotif, unbelief. (4) aperitif

–eeg

(1) gigue, Grieg, klieg, league. (2) blitzkrieg, colleague, fatigue, intrigue.

–eej

(1) liege, siege. (2) besiege, prestige.

–eek

(1) beak, bleak, cheek, chic, creak, creek, eke, freak, geek, Greek, leak, leek, meek, peak, peek, pique, reek, seek, sheik, shriek, Sikh, sleek, sneak, speak, squeak, streak, teak, tweak, weak, week, wreak. (2) antique, bespeak, bezique, cacique, critique, Monique, mystique, oblique, physique, Pike's Peak, unique. (3) Chesapeake, fenugreek, Martinique, Mozambique, winning streak.

–eel

(1) ceil, creel, deal, eel, feel, heal, heel, he'll, keel, kneel, meal, Neal, Neil, peal, peel, real, reel, seal, she'll, spiel, squeal, steal, teal, veal, weal, we'll, wheel, zeal. (2) anneal, appeal, Bastille, cartwheel, Castile, chenille, conceal, congeal, cornmeal, facile, four-wheel, genteel, ideal, Lucille, misdeal, mobile, oatmeal, pastille, repeal, reveal, Tarheel, two-wheel, unreal. (3) Batmobile, chamomile, campanile, cochineal, commonweal, glockenspiel, mercantile, snowmobile. (4) automobile.

–eeld

(1) field, shield, wield, yield. (2) afield, infield, minefield, outfield, Springfield, well-heeled. (3) battlefield, Chesterfield.
ALSO: **–eel** + *-ed* (i.e., *kneeled, appealed*).

–eem

(1) beam, bream, cream, deem, dream, gleam, ream, scheme, scream, seam, seem, steam, stream, team, teem, theme. (2) abeam, beseem, blaspheme, bloodstream, centime, daydream, dream team, esteem, extreme, ice cream, moonbeam, redeem, regime, supreme. (3) academe, self-esteem.

–een

(1) bean, been, clean, dean, Dean, e'en, gene, Gene, glean, green, jean, Jean, keen, lean, lien, mean, mien, peen, preen, quean, queen, scene, screen, seen, sheen, spleen, teen, wean, yean. (2) baleen, beguine, benzene, between, caffeine, canteen, careen, chlorine, Christine, codeine, Colleen, convene, cuisine, demean, demesne, eighteen, Eileen, Eugene, fifteen, foreseen, fourteen, Holstein, Kathleen, machine, marine, nineteen, obscene, Pauline, praline, protein, ravine, routine, saline, sardine, serene, sixteen, thirteen, tureen, unclean. (3) Aberdeen, Abilene, Argentine, atropine, bombazine, brigantine, contravene, crêpe de chine, damascene, evergreen, Florentine, gabardine, gasoline, Geraldine, glycerine, guillotine, intervene, Josephine, kerosene, libertine, maga-

zine, mezzanine, Nazarene, nectarine, nicotine, overseen, Philistine, quarantine, serpentine, seventeen, submarine, tambourine, tangerine, unforeseen, Vaseline, velveteen, wolverine. (4) acetylene, alexandrine, amphetamine, aquamarine, Benedictine, incarnadine.

–aan-**teen**

(3) Byzantine, Levantine. (4) adamantine, elephantine.

–eend

(1) fiend. (2) archfiend.
ALSO: **–een** + -*ed* (i.e., *cleaned, intervened*).

–eep

(1) cheap, cheep, creep, deep, heap, jeep, keep, leap, neap, peep, reap, seep, sheep, sleep, steep, sweep. (2) asleep, upkeep. (3) oversleep. (4) Uriah Heep.

–ees

(1) cease, crease, fleece, geese, grease, Greece, lease, Nice, niece, peace, piece. (2) Bernice, caprice, decease, decrease, increase, hairpiece, Maurice, obese, pelisse, police, release, surcease, valise. (3) altarpiece, diocese, frontispiece, mantelpiece, masterpiece, predecease.

–eesh

(1) leash, quiche. (3) microfiche.

–eest

(1) beast, east, feast, least, priest, yeast. (2) artiste.
ALSO: **–ees** + -*ed* (i.e., *creased, released*).

–eet

(1) beat, beet, bleat, cheat, Crete, eat, feat, feet, fleet, greet, heat, meat, meet, mete, neat, peat, Pete, pleat, seat, sheet, skeet, sleet, street, suite, sweet, teat, treat, wheat. (2) accrete, aesthete, athlete, Backstreet, compete, complete, conceit, concrete, deadbeat, deceit, defeat, delete, deplete, discreet, discrete, effete, elite, entreat, Main Street, petite, receipt, replete, retreat, secrete. (3) bittersweet, Cream of Wheat, incomplete, indiscreet, obsolete, overeat, parakeet.

–eeth

(1) breathe, seethe, sheathe, teethe, wreathe. (2) bequeath, enwreathe.

–eethh

(1) heath, Keith, 'neath, sheath, teeth, wreath. (2) beneath.
(3) underneath.

–eev

(1) breve, cleave, eave, eve, Eve, grieve, heave, leave, lieve, peeve, reeve, sleeve, Steve, thieve, weave, we've. (2) achieve, aggrieve, believe, bereave, conceive, deceive, khedive, naïve, perceive, pet peeve, receive, relieve, reprieve, retrieve. (3) disbelieve, Genevieve, interleave, make-believe, Tel Aviv. (4) overachieve, underachieve.

–eez

(1) breeze, cheese, ease, freeze, frieze, please, seize, sneeze, squeeze, tease, these, wheeze. (2) appease, Aries, Burmese, cerise, chemise, Chinese, disease, displease, Louise, Maltese, Pisces, trapeze. (3) Achilles, antifreeze, Antilles, Balinese, Cantonese, Heloise, Hercules, Japanese, Javanese, journalese, legalese, overseas, Pekinese, Pleiades, Portuguese, Siamese, Socrates, Viennese. (4) antipodes, antitheses, computerese, Hippocrates, hypotheses, parentheses, Vietnamese. (5) Eratosthenes, Mephistopheles.
ALSO: **–ee** + *-s* (i.e., *bees*, *calories*).

–ir-eez

(2) dearies, queries, series, wearies.

–ay-beez

(2) babies, rabies, scabies.

–uhr-meez

(2) Burmese, Hermes, kermes.

–ehb

(1) bleb, deb, Deb, ebb, neb, reb, web. (3) World Wide Web.

–ehch

(1) etch, fetch, ketch, retch, sketch, stretch, vetch, wretch.
(2) outstretch. (3) Etch-A-Sketch.

–ehd

(1) bed, bled, bread, bred, dead, dread, Ed, fed, Fed, fled, Fred, head, Jed, lead, led, Ned, pled, read, red, said, shed, shred, sled, sped, spread, stead, Ted, thread, tread, wed, zed. (2) abed, ahead, airhead, beachhead, bedspread, behead, biped, Club Med, coed, crossbred, deadhead, egghead, forehead, godhead, hogshead, inbred, instead, misled, moped, outspread, unread, unsaid. (3) aforesaid, fountainhead, gingerbread, hammerhead, letterhead, loggerhead, maidenhead, quadruped, sleepyhead, thoroughbred, underfed, watershed.

–ehf

(1) chef, clef, deaf, Jeff. (2) aleph, tone-deaf.

–ehft

(1) cleft, deft, heft, left, theft, weft. (2) bereft.

–ehg

(1) beg, dreg, egg, keg, leg, Meg, peg, Peg. (2) nutmeg, peg leg, powder keg, Winnipeg.

–ehj

(1) dredge, edge, fledge, hedge, kedge, ledge, pledge, sedge, sledge, wedge. (2) allege, on edge.

–ehk

(1) beck, check, cheque, Czech, deck, fleck, heck, neck, peck, speck, tech, trek, wreck. (2) bedeck, henpeck, Quebec, redneck, Star Trek. (3) bottleneck, discotheque, rubberneck, turtleneck.

–ehks

(1) ex, flex, hex, Rex, sex, vex. (2) annex, apex, codex, complex, convex, index, perplex, reflex, Rx, spandex, Tex-Mex. (3) circumflex, multiplex, unisex.
ALSO: **–ek** + *-s* (i.e., *checks*, *henpecks*).

–ohr-**tehks**

(2) cortex, vortex.

–ehkst

(1) next, text. (2) pretext.
ALSO: **–eks** + *-ed* (i.e., *vexed, perplexed*).

–ehkt

(1) sect. (2) abject, affect, bisect, collect, connect, defect, deflect, deject, detect, direct, dissect, effect, eject, elect, erect, expect, infect, inject, inspect, neglect, object, perfect, prefect, project, prospect, protect, reflect, reject, respect, select, subject, suspect. (3) architect, circumspect, dialect, disconnect, disrespect, incorrect, intellect, interject, intersect, introspect, misdirect, recollect, retrospect, vivisect.

ALSO: **–ek** + *-ed* (i.e., *wrecked, bedecked*).

–ehl

(1) bell, belle, Belle, cell, dell, dwell, ell, fell, gel, hell, jell, knell, Nell, quell, sell, shell, smell, spell, swell, tell, well, yell. (2) befell, Boswell, compel, Cornell, dispel, Estelle, excel, Excel, expel, foretell, gazelle, hotel, impel, lapel, pastel, pell-mell, prequel, rebel, repel, sequel. (3) bagatelle, caravel, caramel, citadel, clientele, decibel, hydromel, infidel, Jezebel, muscatel, parallel, personnel, pimpernel, sentinel, undersell, villanelle, William Tell, zinfandel. (4) mademoiselle.

–ehlch

(1) belch, squelch.

–ehld

(1) geld, held, weld. (2) beheld, upheld.

ALSO: **–el** + *-ed* (i.e., *dwelled, impelled*).

–ehlf

(1) elf, pelf, self, shelf. (2) herself, himself, itself, myself, thyself, yourself.

–ehlk

(1) elk, whelk.

–ehlm

(1) elm, helm realm, whelm. (2) overwhelm, underwhelm.

–ehlp

(1) help, kelp, whelp, yelp. (2) self-help.

–ehlt

(1) belt, Celt, dealt, felt, knelt, melt, pelt, smelt, spelt, svelte, veldt, welt. (2) black belt, greenbelt, Sunbelt. (3) Bible Belt.

–ehlthh

(1) health, stealth, wealth. (3) commonwealth.

–ehlv

(1) delve, helve, shelve, twelve.

–ehm

(1) crème, Em, femme, gem, hem, phlegm, stem, them. (2) ahem, condemn, contemn, modem, pro tem, theorem. (3) apothegm, ATM, Bethlehem, diadem, requiem, REM, stratagem.

–ehmpt

(1) dreamt, kempt, tempt. (2) attempt, contempt, exempt, pre-empt, unkempt. (3) tax-exempt.

–ehn

(1) Ben, den, fen, glen, Glenn, Gwen, hen, ken, Ken, men, pen, Seine, ten, then, when, wren, yen, Zen. (2) again, amen, Cheyenne. (3) Adrienne, allergen, citizen, hydrogen, julienne, nitrogen, oxygen, Saracen, specimen. (4) carcinogen, comedienne, equestrienne, tragedienne.

–ehnch

(1) bench, blench, clench, drench, French, mensch, quench, stench, trench, wench, wrench. (2) entrench, retrench. (3) üebermensch.

–ehnd

(1) bend, blend, end, fend, friend, lend, mend, penned, rend, send, spend, tend, trend, vend, wend. (2) amend, append, ascend, attend, befriend, commend, contend, dead end, defend, depend, descend, distend, emend, expend, extend, forefend, impend, intend, misspend, offend, pitchblende, portend, pretend, stipend, suspend, transcend, unbend, weekend. (3) apprehend, comprehend, condescend, dividend, minuend, recommend, reprehend. (4) misapprehend, overextend, superintend.

–ehngth

(1) length, strength. (2) full-length, full-strength.

–ehnj

(2) avenge, revenge, Stonehenge.

–ehns (–ehnts)

(1) cense, cents, dense, dents, fence, gents, hence, pence, rents, scents, sense, tense, tents, thence, vents, whence. (2) accents, ailments, ascents, assents, augments, cements, commence, comments, condense, consents, contents, defense, descents, dispense, dissents, events, expense, ferments, frequents, Hortense, immense, incense, indents, intense, intents, laments, offence, portents, presents, pretense, prevents, relents, repents, resents, suspense, torments. (3) abstinence, accidence, accidents, affluence, ambience, arguments, armaments, audience, battlements, blandishments, chastisements, complements, compliments, condiments, confidence, consequence, consequents, continence, continents, difference, diffidence, diligence, dissidents, documents, elegance, elements, eloquence, eminence, evidence, excellence, filaments, frankincense, governments, immanence, imminence, implements, impotence, impudence, incidence, incidents, increments, indigence, indolence, inference, influence, innocence, instruments, liniments, measurements, monuments, negligence, nutriments, opulence, ornaments, penitence, permanence, precedence, precedents, preference, providence, punishments, recompense, redolence, reference, regiments, represents, residence, reticence, reverence, rudiments, sacraments, sapience, sentiments, settlements, supplements, temperaments, tenements, testaments, truculence, turbulence, vehemence, violence, virulence, wonderments. (4) accomplishments, acknowledgements, advertisements, belligerence, beneficence, benevolence, circumference, developments, embarrassments, establishments, experiments, grandiloquence, impenitence, improvidence, inconsequence, inelegance, intelligence, intransigence, magnificence, munificence, obedience, omnipotence, pre-eminence, presentiments, subservience.

–i-dehns

(2) presidents, residents.

–ehnst

(1) fenced, 'gainst. (2) against, condensed.

–ehnt

(1) bent, cent, dent, gent, Ghent, Kent, leant, lent, Lent, meant, pent, rent, scent, sent, spent, tent, Trent, vent, went. (2) absent, accent, ailment, anent, ascent, assent, augment, cement, comment, consent, content, descent, detent, dissent, event, extent, ferment, foment, frequent, indent, intent, invent, lament, misspent, portent, present, prevent, relent, repent, resent, torment, unbent, unspent. (3) abstinent, accident, argument, armament, banishment, battlement, betterment, blandishment, chastisement, competent, complement, compliment, condiment, confident, consequent, continent, detriment, different, diffident, diligent, dissident, document, element, eloquent, eminent, evident, excellent, exigent, filament, firmament, fraudulent, government, immanent, imminent, implement, impotent, impudent, incident, instrument, languishment, liniment, malcontent, management, measurement, merriment, monument, negligent, nourishment, nutriment, occident, opulent, orient, ornament, overspent, parliament, penitent, permanent, pertinent, precedent, president, prevalent, provident, punishment, ravishment, redolent, regiment, represent, resident, reticent, reverent, rudiment, sacrament, sentiment, settlement, subsequent, succulent, supplement, temperament, tenement, testament, underwent, vehement, violent, virulent, wonderment. (4) accomplishment, acknowledgement, advertisement, astonishment, belligerent, benevolent, development, disarmament, embarrassment, embodiment, enlightenment, environment, establishment, experiment, impenitent, impertinent, imprisonment, improvident, intelligent, irreverent, magnificent, magniloquent, presentiment, subservient. (5) accompaniment.

–ehnz

(1) cleanse, lens. (3) Saracens.
ALSO: **–en** + *-s* (i.e., *hens*, *citizens*).

–ehp

(1) hep, pep, prep, rep, step, steppe, strep, yep. (2) footstep, lockstep, misstep, sidestep. (3) Imhotep.

–ehpt

(1) 'cept, kept, leapt, slept, stepped, swept, wept. (2) accept, adept, except, inept, precept, windswept. (3) intercept, overslept.

–ehr

(1) air, bare, bear, blare, care, chair, Claire, dare, e'er, ere, err, Eyre, fair, fare, flair, flare, glair, glare, hair, hare, heir, Herr, lair, mare, mayor, ne'er, pair, pare, pear, prayer, rare, scare, share, snare, spare, square, stair, stare, swear, tare, tear, their, there, they're, ware, wear, where, yare. (2) affair, armchair, au pair, aware, beware, coheir, compare, corsair, declare, despair, éclair, elsewhere, ensnare, fanfare, forbear, forswear, horsehair, impair, mohair, nightmare, nowhere, outstare, Pierre, prepare, repair, sportswear, unfair, Voltaire, welfare. (3) anywhere, billionaire, debonair, Delaware, doctrinaire, earthenware, étagère, everywhere, laissez faire, legionnaire, luminaire, maidenhair, mal de mer, millionaire, nom de guerre, outerwear, questionnaire, savior faire, solitaire, thoroughfare, unaware, underwear. (4) concessionaire, pied-à-terre, Scarborough Fair.

–ehrd

(1) laird, merde. (2) long-haired. (3) golden-haired.
ALSO: –er + -ed (i.e., *bared*, *ensnared*).

–ehrn

(1) bairn, cairn.

–ehrz

(1) theirs. (2) downstairs, upstairs, unawares.
ALSO: –er + -s (i.e., *airs*, *armchairs*).

–ehs

(1) Bess, bless, chess, cress, dress, guess, jess, Jess, less, mess, press, stress, Tess, tress, yes. (2) abscess, access, actress, address, aggress, assess, caress, compress, confess, countess, depress, digress, distress, duress, empress, excess, express, finesse, impress, ingress, largesse, Loch Ness, mattress, noblesse, obsess, oneness, oppress, possess, princess, profess, progress, recess, redress, repress, success, suppress, transgress, undress, unless. (3) acquiesce, baroness, coalesce, comfortless, convalesce, decompress, dispossess, effervesce, Inverness, obsolesce, overdress, PMS, politesse, repossess, retrogress, sorceress, SOS, wilderness. (4) nevertheless.
ALSO: Words created by addition of suffixes -*less* and -*ness* (i.e., *countless*, *nearness*).

–ee-gres

(2) egress, regress.

–ehsh

(1) crèche, flesh, fresh, mesh, thresh. (2) afresh, enmesh, refresh.
(3) Gilgamesh.

–ehsk

(1) desk. (2) burlesque, grotesque. (3) arabesque, humoresque, Kafkaesque, picturesque, Romanesque, statuesque.

–ehst

(1) best, blest, breast, chest, crest, guest, jest, lest, messed, nest, pest, quest, rest, test, vest, west, wrest, zest. (2) abreast, arrest, attest, behest, bequest, Celeste, congest, contest, detest, digest, divest, incest, infest, ingest, inquest, invest, Key West, molest, protest, request, suggest, unrest. (3) Almagest, anapest, Budapest, Everest, manifest, reinvest, second-best, self-addressed. (4) disinterest.
ALSO: **–es** + *-ed* (i.e., *blessed*, *caressed*).
ALSO: Words created by addition of suffix *-est* (i.e., *easiest*).

–eht

(1) bet, debt, fret, get, jet, let, met, net, pet, Rhett, set, stet, sweat, threat, vet, wet, whet, yet. (2) abet, aigrette, Annette, applet, baguette, barrette, beget, beset, brochette, brunette, cadet, cassette, Claudette, Colette, coquette, corvette, curvet, duet, egret, forget, gazette, Hamlet, Jeannette, octet, offset, omelet, quartet, quintet, regret, rosette, roulette, septet, sestet, sextet, soubrette, sunset, Tibet, upset, vignette. (3) alphabet, amulet, anisette, baronet, bassinet, bayonet, cabinet, calumet, castanet, cigarette, clarinet, coronet, epaulet, epithet, etiquette, Internet, Juliet, marmoset, martinet, mignonette, minaret, minuet, netiquette, parapet, pirouette, quadruplet, space cadet, suffragette, tourniquet, vinaigrette, violet. (4) marionette. (5) audiocassette, videocassette.

–ik-seht

(2) quickset, thickset.

–ehthh

(1) Beth, breath, death, Seth. (2) Macbeth. (3) Elizabeth.

–ehz

(1) fez, says. (2) Suez.

–ei

(1) ay, aye, buy, by, bye, cry, die, dry, dye, eye, fie, fly, fry, guy, Guy, hi, high, I, lie, lye, my, nigh, phi, pi, pie, ply, pry, psi, rye, shy, sigh, sky, sly, spry, spy, sty, Thai, thigh, thy, tie, try, vie, why, wry. (2) ally, apply, awry, Bacchae, Baha'i, belie, bone-dry, bonsai, comply, decry, defy, deny, descry, Eli, espy, GI, goodbye, hereby, imply, knee-high, July, magpie, mudpie, outcry, Popeye, red-eye, rely, reply, sci-fi, semi, Shanghai, shoofly, Sinai, standby, stir fry, supply, thereby, tie-dye, untie, Versailles, whereby. (3) abaci, alibi, alkali, alumni, amplify, beautify, butterfly, by-and-by, certify, citify, clarify, classify, codify, crucify, deify, dignify, edify, falsify, fortify, Gemini, glorify, gratify, horrify, humble pie, hushaby, justify, lazuli, Lorelei, lullaby, magnify, modify, mollify, Mordecai, mortify, multiply, mummify, mystify, nebulae, notify, nullify, occupy, octopi, ossify, pacify, petrify, purify, putrefy, qualify, ratify, rectify, sanctify, stultify, stupefy, terrify, testify, typify, unify, verify, versify, vilify. (4) beatify, declassify, demystify, detoxify, disqualify, diversify, exemplify, humidify, identify, indemnify, intensify, personify, preoccupy, solidify, syllabify. (5) hippopotami. (6) curriculum vitae, modus operandi.

–eib

(1) bribe, gibe, jibe, scribe, tribe. (2) ascribe, describe, imbibe, inscribe, prescribe, proscribe, subscribe, transcribe. (3) circumscribe, diatribe.

–eid

(1) bide, bride, chide, Clyde, glide, guide, hide, Hyde, pride, ride, side, slide, snide, stride, tide, wide. (2) abide, aside, astride, backside, backslide, beside, bedside, bestride, betide, blue-eyed, broadside, bromide, brown-eyed, carbide, cockeyed, collide, confide, cowhide, cross-eyed, decide, deride, divide, elide, green-eyed, hillside, horsehide, inside, misguide, noontide, one-eyed, outside, oxide, preside, provide, reside, seaside, subside, sulfide, sun-dried, wayside, Yuletide, worldwide. (3) alongside, bona fide, coincide, dioxide, eventide, genocide, homicide, iodide, matricide, monoxide, mountainside, open-eyed, override, parricide, peroxide, regicide, subdivide, suicide, underside, waterslide. (4) formaldehyde, infanticide, insecticide, nucleotide.
ALSO: **–ei** + *-ed* (i.e., *cried, beautified*).

–eidz

(1) ides. (2) besides.
ALSO: **–eid** + *-s* (i.e., *chides, confides*).

–eif

(1) fife, knife, life, rife, strife, wife. (2) alewife, half-life, highlife, house-wife, jackknife, lowlife, midlife, midwife. (3) afterlife, Duncan Phyfe.

–eik

(1) bike, dike, hike, like, Mike, pike, psych, spike, strike, tyke. (2) alike, dislike, Klondike, turnpike, unlike, Vandyke.

–eil

(1) aisle, bile, faille, file, guile, I'll, isle, lisle, mile, Nile, pile, rile, smile, stile, style, tile, vile, while, wile. (2) anile, Argyle, awhile, be-guile, compile, defile, erewhile, meanwhile, revile, senile, servile. (3) Anglophile, crocodile, domicile, Francophile, infantile, juvenile, mercantile, puerile, reconcile. (4) bibliophile, Indiophile.

–ehk-seil

(2) exile, flexile.

–ehks-teil

(2) textile. (3) bissextile.

–ehk-teil

(2) sectile. (3) erectile, insectile, projectile.

–ehn-teil

(2) gentile. (3) percentile.

–eild

(1) child, mild, wild, Wilde.
ALSO: –eil + -ed (i.e., *smiled*, *reconciled*).

–eim

(1) chime, chyme, climb, crime, cyme, dime, grime, I'm, lime, mime, prime, rhyme, rime, slime, thyme, time. (2) bedtime, begrime, bedtime, daytime, lifetime, meantime, sometime, springtime, sublime. (3) any-time, Guggenheim, maritime, overtime, pantomime, paradigm, summer-time, wintertime. (4) Nursery Rhyme.

–eimz

(2) ofttimes, sometimes. (3) oftentimes.
ALSO: –eim + -s (i.e., *chimes*, *pantomimes*).

–ein

(1) brine, chine, dine, fine, line, mine, nine, pine, Rhine, shine, shrine, sign, sine, spine, stein, swine, syne, thine, tine, trine, twine, vine, whine, wine. (2) airline, align, assign, benign, bovine, canine, carbine, carmine, crystalline, combine, condign, confine, consign, decline, define, design, divine, enshrine, entwine, grapevine, hircine, incline, lifeline, lupine, mainline, malign, moonshine, opine, outshine, ovine, recline, refine, repine, resign, sunshine, vulpine, woodbine. (3) Adeline, alkaline, anodyne, aquiline, asinine, bottom line, calcimine, calamine, Caroline, Clementine, columbine, concubine, disincline, eglantine, interline, intertwine, iodine, leonine, Liechtenstein, palatine, porcupine, saturnine, serpentine, superfine, timberline, turpentine, underline, undermine, valentine, waterline. (4) elephantine.

–ee-lein

(2) beeline, feline.

–eind

(1) bind, blind, find, grind, hind, kind, mind, rind, wind. (2) behind, mankind, purblind, remind, unkind, unwind. (3) colorblind, humankind, mastermind, womankind.
ALSO: –ein + -ed (i.e., dined, enshrined).

–eip

(1) gripe, pipe, ripe, snipe, stripe, swipe, tripe, type, wipe. (2) bagpipe, blowpipe, hornpipe, peace pipe, sideswipe, unripe, windpipe. (3) archetype, guttersnipe, overripe, prototype. (4) stereotype.

–eir

SEE –ei-uhr.

–eis

(1) Brice, dice, ice, gneiss, lice, mice, nice, price, rice, slice, spice, splice, thrice, trice, twice, vice, vise. (2) advice, allspice, concise, device, entice, precise, suffice. (3) edelweiss, paradise, sacrifice.

–eist

(1) Christ, feist. (2) zeitgeist. (3) poltergeist.
ALSO: –eis + -ed (i.e., diced, sacrificed).

–eit

(1) bight, bite, blight, bright, byte, cite, Dwight, fight, flight, fright, height, kite, knight, light, might, mite, night, plight, quite, right, rite, sight, site, sleight, slight, smite, spite, sprite, tight, trite, white, write. (2) affright, alight, alright, bedight, bobwhite, contrite, daylight, delight, despite, downright, excite, foresight, forthright, goodnight, headlight, Hittite, hoplite, ignite, incite, indict, invite, midnight, moonlight, na-nite, outright, polite, recite, requite, Shiite, starlight, sunlight, tonight, unite, upright, wheelwright. (3) acolyte, aconite, anchorite, anthracite, appetite, Canaanite, candlelight, copyright, disunite, dynamite, erudite, eremite, expedite, Fahrenheit, gesundheit, impolite, kilobyte, neophyte, overnight, oversight, parasite, proselyte, recondite, satellite, stalactite, stalagmite, troglodyte, underwrite, vulcanite, watertight, Yemenite. (4) electrolyte, gemütlichkeit, hermaphrodite, Israelite, meteorite, sub-urbanite, Pre-Raphaelite.

–ei-leit

(2) highlight, skylight, twilight.

–eith

(1) blithe, lithe, scythe, tithe, writhe.

–eiv

(1) chive, Clive, dive, drive, five, gyve, hive, I've, jive, live, rive, shrive, strive, thrive. (2) alive, archive, arrive, beehive, connive, contrive, deprive, derive, nosedive, revive, survive, test-drive. (3) overdrive.

–eiz

(1) guise, prize, rise, size, wise. (2) advise, apprise, arise, assize, baptize, bonsais, capsize, chastise, comprise, demise, despise, devise, disguise, incise, likewise, moonrise, revise, sunrise, surmise, surprise, unwise. (3) advertise, aggrandize, agonize, alkalize, amortize, Anglicize, atomize, authorize, barbarize, bastardize, bowdlerize, brutalize, canalize, canon-ize, carbonize, cauterize, centralize, circumcise, civilize, colonize, com-promise, criticize, crystallize, deputize, dramatize, emphasize, energize, enterprise, equalize, eulogize, euphemize, exercise, exorcise, feminize, fertilize, feudalize, focalize, formalize, fossilize, fraternize, galvanize, harmonize, humanize, hybridize, hypnotize, idolize, immunize, impro-vise, ionize, itemize, jazzercise, jeopardize, legalize, lionize, liquidize, localize, magnetize, maximize, mechanize, memorize, mercerize, mes-merize, methodize, minimize, mobilize, modernize, monetize, moralize,

neutralize, normalize, organize, ostracize, otherwise, oxidize, patronize, penalize, pluralize, polarize, pulverize, realize, recognize, rhapsodize, satirize, scandalize, schematize, scrutinize, sermonize, signalize, socialize, solemnize, specialize, stabilize, standardize, sterilize, stigmatize, subincise, subsidize, summarize, supervise, symbolize, sympathize, symphonize, synchronize, synthesize, systemize, tantalize, televise, temporize, terrorize, theorize, totalize, tranquilize, tyrannize, unionize, utilize, vaporize, verbalize, victimize, vitalize, vocalize, vulcanize, vulgarize, Westernize. (4) acclimatize, actualize, allegorize, alphabetize, anaesthetize, anatomize, antagonize, anthologize, apologize, apostatize, apostrophize, capitalize, characterize, Christianize, commercialize, decentralize, dehumanize, demobilize, democratize, demoralize, deodorize, disorganize, economize, epitomize, extemporize, federalize, generalize, hypothesize, idealize, immobilize, immortalize, italicize, legitimize, liberalize, metabolize, militarize, monopolize, nationalize, naturalize, parenthesize, personalize, philosophize, plagiarize, popularize, prioritize, proselytize, rationalize, regularize, reorganize, ritualize, secularize, singularize, soliloquize, systematize, theologize, theosophize, visualize. (5) Americanize, anathematize, apotheosize, departmentalize, familiarize, legitimatize, materialize, memorialize, particularize, revolutionize, sentimentalize, spiritualize, universalize. (6) Constitutionalize, individualize, institutionalize, intellectualize, internationalize.
ALSO: **–ei** + *-s* (i.e., *sighs, certifies*).

–ib

(1) bib, crib, dib, drib, fib, glib, jib, nib, rib, sib, squib. (2) ad-lib.

–ich

(1) bitch, ditch, flitch, hitch, itch, kitsch, niche, pitch, rich, snitch, stitch, switch, twitch, which, witch. (2) bewitch, enrich, hemstitch, unhitch.

–id

(1) id, bid, Cid, did, grid, hid, kid, lid, mid, quid, rid, skid, slid, squid. (2) amid, David, El Cid, Enid, eyelid, forbid, gravid, Madrid, nonskid, outbid, outdid, Ovid, rabid, undid. (3) arachnid, Captain Kidd, insipid, katydid, overbid, pyramid, underbid.

–ohr-id

(2) florid, forehead, horrid, torrid.

–oo-id

(2) druid, fluid.

–aan-did

(2) banded, candid, handed, landed, stranded. (3) backhanded, high-handed, red-handed, short-handed. (4) empty-handed, even-handed, heavy-handed, single-handed, underhanded.

–aa-lid

(2) ballad, pallid, salad, valid. (3) invalid.

–ah-lid

(2) solid, squalid, stolid.

–oo-mid

(2) fumed, humid, tumid.

–aa-pid

(2) rapid, sapid, vapid.

–eh-pid

(2) tepid, trepid. (3) intrepid.

–aa-sid

(2) acid, flaccid, placid.

–oo-sid

(2) deuced, lucid. (3) pellucid.

–aa-vid

(2) avid, gravid, pavid.

–i-vid

(2) livid, vivid.

–idst

(1) didst, midst. (2) amidst.

–if

(1) biff, cliff, glyph, if, jiff, miff, riff, skiff, sniff, stiff, tiff, whiff.
(2) Heathcliffe, mastiff, midriff, plaintiff, pontiff, Radcliff, serif, sheriff. (3) handkerchief, hieroglyph, hippogriff, san serif.

–ay-lif

(2) bailiff, caliph.

–ift

(1) drift, gift, grift, lift, rift, shift, shrift, sift, swift, thrift. (2) adrift, air-lift, facelift, snowdrift, spendthrift, uplift.
ALSO: **–if** + *-ed* (i.e., *miffed, stiffed*).

–ig

(1) big, brig, dig, fig, gig, jig, pig, prig, rig, sprig, swig, trig, twig, Whig, wig. (2) renege, shindig, jury-rig, periwig, thimblerig, whirligig. (3) thingamajig.

-ij

(1) bridge, midge, ridge. (2) abridge, Cambridge, drawbridge, foot-bridge. (3) acreage, Anchorage, arbitrage, average, beverage, brokerage, equipage, foliage, hemorrhage, heritage, hermitage, lineage, overage, parentage, parsonage, pilgrimage, reportage, tutelage, vicarage.

–ir-ij

(2) clearage, peerage, steerage. (3) arrearage.

–ohr-ij

(2) borage, porridge, storage.

–uhr-ij

(2) courage. (3) demurrage, discourage, encourage.

–ah-lij

(2) college, knowledge. (3) acknowledge, foreknowledge.

–i-lij

(2) grillage, pillage, tillage, village. (3) cartilage, mucilage, privilege, sacrilege.

–i-mij

(2) image, scrimmage.

–eh-sij

(2) message, presage. (3) expressage.

–ah-tij

(2) cottage, pottage, wattage.

–ahr-trij

(2) cartridge, partridge.

–aa-vij

(2) ravage, savage.

–ehr-vij

(2) carriage, marriage. (3) disparage, miscarriage. (4) intermarriage.

-ik

(1) brick, chic, chick, click, clique, crick, dick, Dick, flick, hick, kick, lick, nick, Nick, pick, prick, quick, Rick, sic, sick, slick, snick, stick, thick, tick, trick, Vic, wick. (2) broomstick, carsick, caustic, diptych, goldbrick, heartsick, lovesick, rubric, seasick, sputnik, toothpick, triptych, yardstick. (3) acoustic, bailiwick, bishopric, Bolshevik, candlestick, candlewick, catholic, chivalric, heretic, limerick, lunatic, maverick, myopic, pogo stick, politic, Reykjavik, rhetoric, turmeric. (4) archbishopric, arithmetic, cataleptic, catastrophic, catatonic, impolitic.

–ay-ik

(2) laic. (3) alcaic, Altaic, archaic, deltaic, Hebraic, Judaic, mosaic, Mosaic, Passaic, prosaic, spondaic, trochaic, voltaic. (4) algebraic, Aramaic, pharisaic, Ptolemaic.

–ehr-ik

(2) arrack, barrack, carrack, cleric, Derek, derrick, Erik, ferric. (3) barbaric, chimeric, choleric, enteric, generic, Homeric, hysteric, mesmeric, numeric. (4) climacteric, esoteric, exoteric, isobaric, isomeric, neoteric.

–ir-ik

(2) lyric, pyrrhic, spheric. (3) butyric, chimeric, empiric, satiric. (4) atmospheric, hemispheric, panegyric.

–oh-ik

(2) stoic. (3) azoic, benzoic, heroic. (4) Cenozoic, Mesozoic. (5) Paleozoic.

–ohr-ik

(2) choric, Doric. (3) caloric, euphoric, historic, phosphoric. (4) allegoric, metaphoric, meteoric, paregoric, prehistoric, sophomoric. (5) phantasmagoric.

–uhr-ik

(3) purpuric, sulfuric, telluric.

–oo-bik

(2) cubic, pubic. (3) cherubic.

–aa-dik

(2) nomadic, sporadic.

–ah-dik

(3) anodic, iodic, melodic, methodic, rhapsodic, spasmodic, synodic. (4) episodic, periodic.

–ee-dik

(2) Vedic. (3) comedic. (4) orthopedic. (5) encyclopedic.

–aa-fik

(2) graphic, traffic. (3) seraphic. (4) autographic, biographic, calligraphic, cartographic, chirographic, cosmographic, cryptographic, epigraphic, epitaphic, ethnographic, geographic, holographic, hydrographic, lithographic, monographic, orthographic, pantographic, phonographic, photographic, pornographic, seismographic, stenographic, telegraphic, topographic, typographic, xylographic. (5) bibliographic, choreographic, heliographic, ideographic, lexicographic. (6) autobiographic, cinematographic.

–i-fik

(2) glyphic. (3) deific, horrific, pacific, pontific, prolific, specific, terrific. (4) beatific, calorific, hieroglyphic, honorific, scientific, soporific.

–aa-jik

(2) magic, tragic. (3) pelagic.

–aa-lik

(2) Alec, Gallic, malic, phallic, salic. (3) cephalic, italic, metallic, oxalic, vocalic.

–ah-lik

(2) colic, frolic, rollick. (3) bucolic, carbolic, embolic, symbolic, systolic. (4) alcoholic, apostolic, diastolic, diabolic, hyperbolic, melancholic, metabolic, vitriolic.

–aw-lik

(3) hydraulic. (4) alcoholic.

–eh-lik

(2) melic, relic, telic. (3) angelic. (4) archangelic, evangelic, philatelic.

–ah-mik

(2) comic, gnomic. (3) atomic. (4) agronomic, anatomic, astronomic, autonomic, diatomic, economic, monatomic, taxonomic.

–ee-mik

(3) anemic, graphemic, morphemic, phonemic, toxemic.
(4) epistemic.

–eh-mik

(2) chemic. (3) alchemic, endemic, pandemic, polemic, systemic, totemic. (4) academic, epidemic.

–i-mik

(2) gimmick, mimic. (4) eponymic, homonymic, matronymic, metonymic, pantomimic, patronymic, synonymic.

–aa-nik

(2) manic, panic, tannic. (3) botanic, Britannic, galvanic, Germanic, mechanic, organic, satanic, titanic, Titanic, volcanic, volcanic. (4) aldermanic, charlatanic, Messianic, oceanic, talismanic.

–ah-nik

(2) chronic, chthonic, conic, phonic, sonic, tonic. (3) agonic, bubonic, Byronic, canonic, carbonic, colonic, cyclonic, demonic, draconic, euphonic, harmonic, hedonic, ionic, ironic, laconic, Masonic, mnemonic, platonic, sardonic, Slavonic, symphonic, tectonic, Teutonic. (4) diaphonic, diatonic, electronic, embryonic, histrionic, hydroponic, isotonic, monophonic, philharmonic, polyphonic, Solomonic, telephonic, ultrasonic. (5) architectonic, stereophonic.

–ee-nik

(2) scenic. (3) irenic.

–eh-nik

(2) phrenic. (3) arsenic, Edenic, eugenic, Hellenic, hygienic, irenic, splenic. (4) allergenic, callisthenic, neurasthenic, Panhellenic, pathogenic, photogenic, psychogenic, schizophrenic, telegenic. (5) carcinogenic. (6) hallucinogenic.

–i-nik

(2) clinic, cynic. (3) actinic, rabbinic. (4) Jacobinic.

–oo-nik

(2) Munich, Punic, runic, tunic.

–ah-pik

(2) topic, tropic. (3) myopic. (4) microscopic, misanthropic, philanthropic, presbyopic, spectroscopic, telescopic. (5) heliotropic, kaleidoscopic, stereoscopic.

–aa-sik

(2) classic. (3) Jurassic, thoracic, Triassic.

–aw-stik

(2) caustic, Gnostic. (3) acrostic, agnostic, prognostic. (4) diagnostic.

–aa-tik

(2) attic, static. (3) aquatic, asthmatic, chromatic, climatic, Dalmatic, dogmatic, dramatic, ecstatic, emphatic, erratic, fanatic, hepatic, lymphatic, phlegmatic, pneumatic, pragmatic, prismatic, quadratic, rheumatic, Socratic, stigmatic, thematic, traumatic. (4) achromatic, acrobatic, Adriatic, aerostatic, aromatic, Asiatic, autocratic, automatic, bureaucratic, democratic, dichromatic, diplomatic, emblematic, enigmatic, hieratic, hydrostatic, mathematic, morganatic, numismatic, operatic, pancreatic, plutocratic, problematic, symptomatic, systematic. (5) anagrammatic, aristocratic, axiomatic, epigrammatic, idiomatic, melodramatic, psychosomatic, undiplomatic. (6) idiosyncratic.

–aak-tik

(2) lactic, tactic. (3) climactic, didactic, galactic, syntactic. (4) prophylactic. (5) anticlimactic.

–aan-tik

(2) antic, frantic, mantic. (3) Atlantic, bacchantic, gigantic, pedantic, romantic. (4) corybantic, geomantic, hydromantic, necromantic, sycophantic, transatlantic. (5) hierophantic.

–aas-tik

(2) drastic, mastic, plastic, spastic. (3) bombastic, dynastic, elastic, fantastic, gymnastic, monastic, sarcastic, scholastic. (4) antiphrastic, chiliastic, inelastic, orgiastic, paraphrastic, periphrastic, pleonastic. (5) ecclesiastic, enthusiastic, iconoclastic.

–ah-tik

(3) chaotic, demonic, despotic, erotic, exotic, hypnotic, narcotic, neurotic, osmotic, pyretic, quixotic. (4) idiotic, patriotic. (5) macrobiotic, microbiotic.

–ahp-tik

(2) Coptic, optic. (3) synoptic.

–eh-tik

(3) aesthetic, ascetic, athletic, balletic, bathetic, cosmetic, emetic, frenetic, genetic, hermetic, kinetic, magnetic, mimetic, pathetic, phonetic, phrenetic, poetic, prophetic, splenetic, synthetic. (4) alphabetic, analgetic, anaesthetic, antihetic, apathetic, arithmetic, dietetic, energetic, exegetic, geodetic, homiletic, hypothetic, parenthetic, sympathetic, theoretic. (5) antipathetic, biogenetic, peripatetic. (6) unapologetic, onomatopoetic.

–ehk-tik

(2) hectic, pectic. (3) cachectic, eclectic. (4) analectic, anorectic, apoplectic, catalectic, dialectic.

–ehn-tik

(3) authentic, identic.

–ehp-tik

(2) peptic, septic, skeptic. (3) aseptic, dyspeptic, eupeptic. (4) antiseptic, cataleptic, epileptic.

–ehs-tik

(3) domestic, majestic. (4) anapestic, catachrestic.

–i-tik

(2) critic. (3) arthritic, bronchitic, dendritic, Hamitic, mephitic, proclitic, rachitic, Semitic. (4) analytic, biolytic, catalytic, cenobitic, eremitic, Jesuitic, paralytic, parasitic. (5) meteoritic. (6) psychoanalytic.

–ip-tik

(2) cryptic, diptych, glyptic, styptic, triptych. (3) ecliptic, elliptic. (4) apocalyptic.

–is-tik

(2) cystic, fistic, mystic. (3) artistic, ballistic, deistic, juristic, linguistic, logistic, puristic, sadistic, simplistic, sophistic, statistic, stylistic, theistic, touristic. (4) altruistic, anarchistic, animistic, atavistic, atheistic, Bolshevistic, cabalistic, casuistic, catechistic, chauvinistic, communistic, egoistic, egotistic, euphemistic, fatalistic, humanistic, journalistic, nihilistic, optimistic, pantheistic, pessimistic, pietistic, pugilistic, realistic, socialistic, solecistic, syllogistic. (5) anachronistic, capitalistic, characteristic, idealistic, polytheistic, rationalistic, ritualistic, sensualistic. (6) materialistic, spiritualistic. (7) individualistic.

–oo-tik

(3) scorbutic. (4) hermeneutic, therapeutic.

–uhs-tik

(2) fustic, rustic.

–ehn-trik

(2) centric. (3) acentric, concentric, eccentric. (4) geocentric. (5) anthropocentric, heliocentric.

–i-zik

(2) phthisic, physic. (3) metaphysic.

–iks

(1) fix, mix, nix, six, Styx. (2) admix, affix, commix, infix, matrix, onyx, prefix, prolix, suffix, transfix, unfix. (3) cicatrix, crucifix, fiddlesticks, intermix. (4) double helix, executrix. (5) archaeopteryx.
ALSO: –ik + -s (i.e., *kicks, yardsticks*).

–ee-liks

(2) Felix, helix.

–aa-niks

(2) annex, panics. (3) mechanics.

–ikst

(1) twixt. (2) betwixt.
ALSO: **–iks** + *-ed* (i.e., *mixed*, *transfixed*).

–ikt

(1) strict. (2) addict, afflict, conflict, constrict, convict, depict, edict, evict, inflict, predict, restrict. (3) Benedict, contradict, derelict, interdict.
ALSO: **–ik** + *-ed* (i.e., *clicked*, *tricked*).

–il

(1) bill, Bill, chill, dill, drill, fill, frill, gill, grill, hill, ill, Jill, kill, mill, nil, Phil, pill, quill, rill, shill, shrill, sill, skill, spill, still, swill, thrill, 'til, till, trill, twill, 'twill, will, Will. (2) Brazil, distill, downhill, fulfill, instill, quadrille, Seville, treadmill, uphill. (3) chlorophyll, codicil, daffodil, espadrille, imbecile, Louisville, versatile, volatile, whippoorwill.

–ilch

(1) filch, milch, zilch.

–ild

(1) billed, build, chilled, drilled, filled, frilled, gild, grilled, guild, killed, milled, skilled, spilled, swilled, thrilled, tilled, willed. (2) distilled, fulfilled, instilled.
ALSO: **–il** + *-ed* (i.e., *chilled*, *instilled*).

-ilk

(1) bilk, ilk, milk, silk.

-ilt

(1) built, gilt, guilt, hilt, jilt, kilt, lilt, milt, quilt, silt, spilt, stilt, tilt, wilt. (2) atilt, rebuilt. (3) Vanderbilt.

-ilth

(1) filth, tilth.

-im

(1) brim, dim, Grimm, gym, him, hymn, Jim, Kim, limb, limn, prim, rim, shim, skim, slim, swim, Tim, trim, vim, whim. (2) bedim, prelim, Purim. (3) acronym, antonym, cherubim, eponym, homonym, interim, pseudonym, seraphim, synonym.

–imp

(1) blimp, chimp, crimp, gimp, guimpe, imp, limp, pimp, primp, scrimp, shrimp, skimp, wimp.

–imps

(1) glimpse.

ALSO: –imp + -s (i.e., *chimps*, *skimps*).

–in

(1) been, bin, chin, din, fin, Finn, gin, grin, in, inn, jinn, kin, Lynn, pin, shin, sin, skin, spin, thin, tin, twin, win. (2) akin, bearskin, begin, Berlin, bowfin, Brooklyn, buckskin, chagrin, Corinne, dragon, herein, merkin, sidespin, tailspin, therein, wagon. (3) alkaline, aniline, aquiline, aspirin, crinoline, discipline, endorphin, feminine, gelatin, genuine, glycerin, harlequin, heroine, Jacobin, javelin, jessamine, mandarin, mandolin, mannequin, masculine, moccasin, paladin, peregrine, saccharine, sibylline, violin, Zeppelin. (4) adrenaline. (5) nitroglycerine.

ALSO: Contractions/distortions ending in -*in'* (i.e., *singin'*).

–inch

(1) chinch, cinch, clinch, finch, flinch, inch, lynch, pinch, winch.
(2) chaffinch, goldfinch, twelve-inch.

–ind

(1) finned, grinned, pinned, sinned, skinned, wind. (2) chagrined, rescind, whirlwind, woodwind. (3) disciplined, tamarind.

ALSO: –in + -*ed* (i.e., *grinned*, *chagrined*).

–ing

(1) bing, bring, cling, ding, fling, king, Ming, ping, ring, sing, sling, spring, sting, string, swing, thing, wing, wring, ying. (2) changeling, evening, hireling, mainspring, O-ring, plaything, something, unstring. (3) anything, atheling, everything, opening, underling.

ALSO: Words created by addition of suffix -*ing* (i.e., *singing*).

–ahng-ing (–awng-ing)

(2) longing, thronging, wronging. (3) belonging, prolonging.

–ehr-ing

(2) airing, bearing, caring, daring, erring, fairing, glaring, herring, raring, sparing, wearing. (3) seafaring, uncaring, unsparing, wayfaring. (4) overbearing.

–ir-ing

(2) blearing, cheering, clearing, earring, fearing, fleering, gearing, hearing, jeering, leering, nearing, peering, rearing, searing, shearing, smearing, sneering, spearing, steering, tearing, veering. (3) adhering, appearing, cashiering, cohering, endearing, God-fearing, inhering, revering. (4) auctioneering, commandeering, disappearing, domineering, engineering, hard-of-hearing, interfering, overhearing, persevering, pioneering, profiteering, volunteering.

–oh-ing

(2) blowing, crowing, flowing, glowing, going, growing, knowing, lowing, mowing, owing, rowing, sewing, showing, snowing, sowing, stowing, towing, throwing. (3) mind-blowing, seagoing.

–aan-ding

(2) banding, branding, landing, standing. (3) demanding, disbanding, expanding, outstanding, upstanding. (4) notwithstanding, understanding.

–ah-ding

(2) nodding, plodding, prodding, wadding.

–eh-ding

(2) bedding, dreading, heading, shedding, shredding, sledding, spreading, threading, wedding.

–ehl-ding

(2) gelding, melding, welding.

–ehn-ding

(2) pending.
ALSO: –end + -ing (i.e., *blending, amending*).

–i-ding

(2) bidding, kidding, ridding.

–il-**ding**

(2) building, gilding. (3) rebuilding.

–uu-**ding**

(2) hooding, pudding.

–uh-**fing**

(2) bluffing, cuffing, huffing, puffing, stuffing.

–ei-**king**

(2) biking, diking, hiking, liking, piking, spiking, striking, Viking. (3) disliking.

–aant-**ling**

(2) bantling, mantling, scantling. (3) dismantling.

–aap-**ling**

(2) dappling, grappling, sapling.

–aat-**ling**

(2) battling, fatling, Gatling, rattling, tattling.

–ahd-**ling**

(2) coddling, codling, godling, modeling, swaddling, toddling, twaddling, waddling.

–ahr-**ling**

(2) darling, marling, snarling, starling.

–ahrk-**ling**

(2) darkling, sparkling.

–ay-**ling**

(2) ailing, failing, grayling, paling.

–eed-**ling**

(2) needling, seedling, wheedling.

–eif-**ling**

(2) rifling, stifling, trifling.

–i-**ling**

(2) billing, shilling, willing. (3) unwilling.
ALSO: **–il** + -*ing* (i.e., *milling*).

–ib-**ling**

(2) dibbling, dribbling, nibbling, quibbling, scribbling, sibling.

–id-**ling**

(2) fiddling, middling, piddling, riddling, twiddling.

–ink-**ling**

(2) crinkling, inkling, sprinkling, tinkling, twinkling, winkling, wrinkling.

–ip-**ling**

(2) crippling, Kipling, rippling, stippling, tippling.

–uhk-**ling**

(2) buckling, duckling, suckling.

–uhr-**ling**

(2) curling, furling, hurling, purling, skirling, sterling, swirling, twirling, whirling.

–ahr-**ming**

(2) arming, charming, farming. (3) alarming, disarming.

–ei-**ming**

(2) chiming, climbing, liming, priming, rhyming, timing.

–i-**ming**

(2) brimming, dimming, skimming, slimming, swimming, trimming.

–aw-**ning**

(2) awning, dawning, fawning, spawning, yawning.

–ee-**ning**

(2) cleaning, gleaning, leaning, meaning, preening, screening, weaning. (3) careening, convening, demeaning, machining. (4) contravening, intervening.

–ei-**ning**

SEE: –**ein** + -*ing* (i.e., *dining*, *aligning*).

–eit-**ning**

(3) brightening, frightening, lightening, tightening, whitening.

–ohr-ning

(2) morning, mourning, scorning, warning. (3) adorning, forewarning.

–uhr-ning

(2) burning, churning, earning, learning, spurning, turning, yearning. (3) concerning, discerning, returning.

–ah-ping

(2) chopping, sopping, topping, whopping. (3) eye-popping, name-dropping. (4) window-shopping.

–ee-sing

(2) fleecing. (3) increasing, subleasing.

–eh-sing

(2) blessing, dressing, guessing, pressing.
ALSO: –es + -ing (i.e., *confessing*)

–aas-ting

(2) blasting, casting, fasting, lasting. (3) broadcasting, contrasting, forecasting, miscasting. (4) everlasting, flabbergasting, telecasting.

–ehn-ting

(2) denting, renting, scenting, tenting, venting. (3) absenting, accenting, assenting, augmenting, cementing, consenting, fermenting, fomenting, frequenting, lamenting, presenting, preventing, relenting, resenting, tormenting. (4) circumventing, complementing, complimenting, ornamenting, representing, supplementing. (5) misrepresenting.

–ei-ting

(2) biting, whiting. (3) handwriting.
ALSO: –eit + -ing (lighting, inciting, indicting).

–i-ting

(2) fitting, flitting, fritting, gritting, hitting, knitting, pitting, quitting, sitting, slitting, spitting, witting. (3) hair-splitting, unwitting.

–ee-thing

(2) breathing, seething, sheathing, teething, wreathing.
(3) bequeathing, fire-breathing.

–ei-**thing**

(2) scything, tithing, writhing.

–oh-**thing**

(2) clothing, loathing.

–ahr-**ving**

(2) carving, starving.

–ehl-**ving**

(2) delving, helving, shelving.

–ee-**zing**

(2) breezing, easing, freezing, pleasing, sneezing, squeezing, teasing. (3) appeasing, displeasing, refreezing, unpleasing.

–ink

(1) blink, brink, chink, clink, drink, fink, ink, kink, link, mink, pink, rink, shrink, sink, skink, slink, stink, think, wink, zinc. (2) doublethink, hoodwink, lip-sync. (3) bobolink, Humperdinck, interlink.

–inks

(1) jinx, lynx, minx, sphinx. (2) larynx, methinks. (3) tiddlywinks.
ALSO: **–ink** + *-s* (i.e., *blinks*, *interlinks*).

–inkt

(2) distinct, extinct, instinct, precinct, succinct. (3) indistinct.
ALSO: **–ink** + *-ed* (i.e., *winked*, *lip-synced*).

–ins

(1) blintz, chintz, mince, prince, quince, rinse, since, wince.
(2) convince, evince.

–int

(1) dint, flint, glint, hint, lint, mint, print, quint, splint, sprint, squint, stint, tint. (2) asquint, footprint, imprint, misprint, Peer Gynt, reprint, spearmint. (3) aquatint, peppermint.

–inthh

(1) plinth. (2) absinthe, Corinth. (3) hyacinth, labyrinth.

–ip

(1) blip, chip, clip, dip, drip, flip, grip, grippe, gyp, hip, kip, lip, nip, pip, quip, rip, scrip, ship, sip, skip, slip, snip, strip, tip, trip, whip, yip, zip. (2) airstrip, catnip, cowslip, equip, flagship, horsewhip, lightship, outstrip, transship, unzip, V-chip. (3) battleship, ego trip, fellowship, marksmanship, microchip, scholarship, showmanship, weatherstrip.
ALSO: Words created by addition of suffix -ship (i.e., *friendship*).

–ips

(2) eclipse, ellipse. (3) apocalypse.
ALSO: **–ip** + -s (i.e., *drips, flagships*).

–ipt

(1) crypt, script. (2) conscript, encrypt, postscript, transcript.
ALSO: **–ip** + -ed (i.e., *quipped, outstripped*).

–ir

(1) beer, bier, blear, cheer, clear, dear, deer, drear, ear, fear, fleer, gear, hear, here, jeer, Lear, leer, mere, near, peer, pier, queer, rear, sear, seer, sere, shear, sheer, smear, sneer, spear, sphere, steer, tear, tier, veer, weir, year. (2) adhere, ampere, appear, arrear, austere, brassiere, career, cashier, cashmere, cohere, compeer, emir, endear, frontier, inhere, Kashmir, reindeer, revere, severe, sincere, Tangier, veneer. (3) atmosphere, auctioneer, bandoleer, bombardier, brigadier, buccaneer, cavalier, chandelier, chanticleer, chiffonier, commandeer, disappear, domineer, engineer, financier, gazetteer, gondolier, grenadier, Guinevere, hemisphere, insincere, interfere, mountaineer, muleteer, musketeer, overhear, pamphleteer, persevere, pioneer, privateer, profiteer, souvenir, stratosphere, troposphere, volunteer. (4) charioteer, electioneer.

–ird

(1) beard, cheered, cleared, feared, geared, jeered, leered, peered, sheared, smeared, sneered, speared, tiered, weird. (2) adhered, afeard, appeared, cohered, dog-eared, revered, veneered. (3) commandeered, disappeared, domineered, engineered, interfered, persevered, pioneered, volunteered.

–irs

(1) fierce, pierce, tierce. (2) transpierce.

–is

(1) bliss, Chris, dis, hiss, kiss, miss, Swiss, this. (2) abyss, amiss, crevice, dismiss, grimace, jaundice, remiss, solstice. (3) ambergris, armistice, artifice, avarice, Beatrice, benefice, chrysalis, cowardice, edifice, emphasis, genesis, nemesis, orifice, precipice, prejudice, synthesis, verdigris. (4) acropolis, anabasis, analysis, antithesis, dieresis, hypothesis, metropolis, necropolis, paralysis, parenthesis, rigor mortis. (5) metamorphosis.

–aa-lis

(2) Alice, callous, chalice, Dallas, malice, palace, Pallas, phallus, talus, thallus. (4) borealis, digitalis. (7) aurora borealis.

–ehn-tis

(3) apprentice, momentous, portentous.

–ish

(1) dish, fish, knish, squish, swish, wish. (2) blowfish, bluefish, catfish, flatfish, goldfish, whitefish, whitish. (3) angelfish, babyish, devilfish, devilish, feverish, flying fish, gibberish, kittenish, microfiche. (4) impoverish.
ALSO: Words created by addition of suffix -ish (i.e., *childish*).

–ehr-ish

(2) bearish, cherish, garish, parish, perish.

–ohr-ish

(2) boarish, boorish, Moorish, whorish.

–oo-ish

(2) blueish, Jewish, shrewish.

–uhr-ish

(2) currish, flourish, nourish.

–uh-bish

(2) clubbish, cubbish, rubbish.

–aa-dish

(2) baddish, caddish, faddish, radish.

–aan-dish

(2) blandish, brandish, Standish. (3) outlandish.

–eil-dish

(2) childish, wildish.

–ahr-fish

(2) garfish, starfish.

–ehl-fish

(2) elfish, selfish, shellfish. (3) unselfish.

–aa-gish

(2) haggish, waggish.

–aw-gish

(2) doggish, hoggish.

–aang-gwish

(2) anguish, languish.

–aa-kish

(2) blackish, brackish.

–ahr-kish

(2) darkish, larkish.

–ah-lish

(2) polish. (3) abolish, demolish.

–eh-lish

(2) hellish, relish. (3) embellish.

–oo-lish

(2) foolish, mulish.

–uhr-lish

(2) churlish, girlish.

–ee-mish

(2) beamish, squeamish.

–eh-mish

(2) blemish, Flemish.

–uhr-mish

(2) skirmish, squirmish.

–aa-nish

(2) banish, clannish, mannish, Spanish, vanish.

–ah-nish

(2) donnish, wannish. (3) admonish, astonish, premonish.

–ahr-nish

(2) garnish, tarnish, varnish.

–eh-nish

(2) plenish, Rhenish. (3) replenish.

–ei-nish

(2) brinish, swinish.

–i-nish

(2) finish, Finnish, thinnish. (3) diminish, refinish.

–uhr-nish

(2) burnish, furnish.

–uhm-pish

(2) dumpish, frumpish, lumpish, plumpish.

–ah-tish

(2) schottische, Scottish, sottish.

–eh-tish

(2) fetish, pettish. (3) coquettish.

–ohl-tish

(2) coltish, doltish.

–uh-tish

(2) ruttish, sluttish.

–aa-vish

(2) lavish, ravish.

–ee-vish

(2) peevish, thievish.

–isk

(1) bisque, brisk, disc, disk, frisk, risk, whisk. (3) asterisk, basilisk, obelisk, odalisque, tamarisk. (4) videodisk.

–isp

(1) crisp, lisp, wisp. (4) will o' the wisp.

–ist

(1) cist, cyst, fist, gist, grist, list, mist, schist, tryst, twist, whist, wrist. (2) assist, blacklist, chemist, consist, Cubist, cyclist, desist, druggist, duelist, enlist, entwist, exist, faddist, Fascist, flautist, harpist, insist, linguist, monist, persist, resist, sophist, stylist, subsist, Taoist, typist. (3) alarmist, Alpinist, amethyst, archivist, bicyclist, catechist, coexist, copyist, egotist, essayist, extremist, fetishist, futurist, guitarist, liturgist, machinist, mesmerist, modernist, occultist, pacifist, portraitist, pre-exist, pyrrhonist, re-enlist, reservist, satirist, sitarist, trombonist. (4) clarinetist, equilibrist, metallurgist, propagandist, protectionist, taxidermist, telepathist, theosophist, violinist.
ALSO: –is + -ed (i.e., *kissed, jaundiced*).

–ay-ist

(3) Hebraist, Judaist. (4) algebraist.

–ee-ist

(2) deist, theist. (3) atheist, copyist, hobbyist, lobbyist, pantheist. (4) monotheist, polytheist.

–ir-ist

(2) dearest, lyrist, nearest.

–oh-ist

(3) banjoist, egoist, Shintoist, soloist.

–ohr-ist

(2) florist, forest, sorest. (3) aorist, amorist, aphorist, folklorist, meliorist, theorist.

–oo-ist

(2) cueist. (3) altruist, canoeist, euphuist.

–uhr-ist

(3) armorist, colorist, diarist, Eucharist, humorist, motorist, terrorist, zitherist. (4) apiarist, militarist, plagiarist, secularist.

–uur-ist

(2) jurist, purist, tourist. (4) manicurist. (5) agriculturist, caricaturist, floriculturist, horticulturist, miniaturist.

–ah-dist

(2) bodiced, modest, oddest. (3) immodest.

–oo-dist

(2) Buddhist, crudest, feudist, lewdest, nudist, rudest, shrewdest.

–uh-dist

(3) Methodist, rhapsodist, Talmudist. (4) chiropodist.

–ah-luh-jist

(4) anthologist, apologist, biologist, ethnologist, geologist, horologist, monologist, neoligist, pathologist, phrenologist, psychologist, theologist. (5) anthropologist, archeologist, dermatologist, Egyptologist, entomologist, etymologist, genealogist, gynecologist, mineralogist, ophthalmologist, pharmacologist, physiologist. (6) bacteriologist.

–uh-jist

(3) elegist, eulogist, strategist, suffragist.

–ahr-kist

(3) anarchist, monarchist.

–oh-kist

(2) focused, locust.

–uh-kwist

(3) colloquist. (4) soliloquist, ventriloquist.

–oo-list

(3) fabulist, oculist. (4) somnambulist.

–uh-list

(3) annalist, analyst, catalyst, centralist, cymbalist, dualist, fatalist, feudalist, formalist, herbalist, homilist, journalist, legalist, loyalist, medallist, moralist, nihilist, novelist, pluralist, pugilist, realist, specialist, symbolist, violist, vocalist. (4) capitalist, clericalist, communalist, enamellist, Evangelist, Federalist, idealist, liberalist, literalist, monopolist, nominalist, philatelist, rationalist, revivalist, ritualist, sensualist. (5) commercialist, conceptualist, imperialist, medievalist, Occidentalist, Orientalist, phenomenalist, sacerdotalist, spiritualist, traditionalist, transcendentalist, universalist. (6) ceremonialist, Congregationalist, constitutionalist, controversialist, conversationalist, educationalist, experimentalist, individualist, institutionalist, internationalist, supernaturalist.

–ahl-mist

(2) calmest, palmist, psalmist.

–ohr-mist

(3) conformist, reformist. (4) nonconformist.

–uh-mist

(3) alchemist, animist, atomist, bigamist, optimist, pessimist. (4) agronomist, anatomist, autonomist, economist, legitimist, monogamist, polygamist, taxonomist.

–ah-nist

(2) honest, wannest. (3) dishonest.

–ee-nist

(4) magazinist.
ALSO: –een + -ist (i.e., *meanest, greenest*).

–im-nist

(4) gymnast, hymnist.

–oo-nist

(3) balloonist, cartoonist, lampoonist. (4) opportunist.

–uh-nist

(3) botanist, colonist, Calvinist, Darwinist, factionist, fictionist, hedonist, Hellenist, humanist, hygienist, Latinist, mechanist, organist, pianist, Platonist, Romanist, shamanist, Stalinist, unionist, Zionist. (4) accompanist, alienist, antagonist, contortionist, determinist, exclusionist, expressionist, extortionist, illusionist, impressionist, misogynist, obstructionist, perfectionist, protagonist, religionist, revisionist, Salvationist, tobacconist. (5) abolitionist, elocutionist, evolutionist, insurrectionist, oppositionist, post-impressionist, prohibitionist, revolutionist, vivisectionist.

–uhr-nist

(2) earnest, Ernest, sternest. (3) internist.

–aan-thruh-pist

(4) misanthropist, philanthropist.

–ay-pist

(2) papist, rapist. (3) escapist, landscapist.

–uh-sist

(3) biblicist, classicist, pharmacist, physicist, publicist.
(4) polemicist.

–aan-tist

(3) Vedantist. (4) obscurantist.

–aap-tist

(2) aptest, Baptist. (4) Anabaptist.

–ahr-tist

(2) artist, chartist, smartest.

–ehn-tist

(2) dentist, prenticed. (3) Adventist, apprenticed.

–oo-tist

(2) cutest, flutist. (4) absolutist, parachutist.

–uh-tist

(3) dogmatist, dramatist, hypnotist, librettist, nepotist, pragmatist, scientist, separatist.

–uh-**trist**

(4) optometrist, psychiatrist.

–uh-**vist**

(3) Bolshevist. (4) collectivist, negativist, objectivist, positivist, recidivist.

–it

(1) bit, chit, fit, flit, grit, hit, it, kit, knit, lit, mitt, nit, pit, quit, sit, skit, slit, spit, split, sprit, tit, twit, whit, wit, writ, zit. (2) acquit, admit, armpit, befit, biscuit, bowsprit, commit, emit, forfeit, hobbit, misfit, moonlit, omit, outwit, permit, refit, remit, respite, starlit, submit, sunlit, surfeit, tidbit, tomtit, transmit, unfit. (3) apposite, benefit, counterfeit, definite, favorite, hypocrite, infinite, Inuit, Jesuit, opposite. (4) indefinite.

–eh-**dit**

(2) credit, edit. (3) accredit, discredit. (4) copyedit.

–aas-**kit**

(2) basket, casket, flasket, gasket.

–ah-**mit**

(2) comet, grommet, vomit.

–i-**zit**

(3) exquisite, perquisite, requisite. (4) prerequisite.

–ith

(1) kith, myth, pith, smith, with. (2) blacksmith, Edith, forthwith, herewith, therewith, wherewith, zenith. (3) acrolith, Aerosmith, monolith, silversmith.

–itz

(1) blitz, ditz, Fritz, it's, Ritz, spitz.

ALSO: –it + -s (i.e., *fits*, *omits*).

–iv

(1) give, live, sieve. (2) costive, forgive, outlive, plaintive, relive.
(3) absorptive, adoptive, combustive, concoctive, exhaustive,
expansive, reflexive, responsive, substantive.

–aa-siv

(2) massive, passive. (3) impassive.

–ay-siv

(3) abrasive, assuasive, dissuasive, evasive, invasive, persuasive,
pervasive.

–ee-siv

(3) adhesive, cohesive.

–eh-siv

(3) aggressive, compressive, concessive, depressive, digressive,
excessive, expressive, impressive, obsessive, oppressive, posses-
sive, progressive, recessive, regressive, repressive, successive,
suppressive, transgressive. (4) inexpressive, retrogressive. (5)
manic-depressive.

–ehn-siv

(2) pensive, tensive. (3) ascensive, defensive, expensive, extensive,
intensive, offensive, ostensive, protensive, suspensive. (4) appre-
hensive, coextensive, comprehensive, hypertensive, inexpensive,
inoffensive, reprehensive. (5) incomprehensive, labor-intensive.

–ei-siv

(3) decisive, derisive, divisive, incisive. (4) indecisive.

–i-siv

(3) missive, dismissive, permissive, remissive, submissive.

–oh-siv

(3) corrosive, erosive, explosive, implosive, purposive.

–oo-siv

(3) abusive, allusive, collusive, conclusive, conducive, delusive,
diffusive, effusive, exclusive, illusive, inclusive, infusive, intrusive,
obtrusive, preclusive, protrusive, reclusive, seclusive. (4) all-inclu-
sive, inconclusive.

–uh-siv

(3) concussive, percussive. (4) repercussive.

–uhl-siv

(3) compulsive, convulsive, divulsive, expulsive, impulsive, propulsive, repulsive, revulsive.

–uhr-siv

(2) cursive. (3) coercive, discursive, excursive, incursive, subversive.

–aak-tiv

(2) active. (3) abstractive, attractive, coactive, contractive, detractive, distractive, enactive, inactive, proactive, reactive, refractive, subtractive. (4) counteractive, putrefactive, retroactive. (5) radioactive.

–aap-tiv

(2) captive (3) adaptive.

–ay-tiv

(2) dative, native. (3) creative, dilative. (4) aggregative, cogitative, combinative, compensative, connotative, contemplative, corporative, denotative, designative, educative, emulative, estimative, exhortative, generative, hesitative, imitative, innovative, integrative, legislative, meditative, predicative, procreative, qualitative, quantitative, regulative, ruminative, terminative, vegetative. (5) administrative, agglutinative, assimilative, authoritative, continuative, corroborative, determinative, discriminative, exonerative, illuminative, investigative, premeditative.

–ehk-tiv

(3) adjective, affective, collective, connective, corrective, defective, deflective, detective, directive, effective, elective, erective, infective, inflective, injective, invective, objective, perfective, perspective, projective, prospective, protective, reflective, rejective, respective, selective, subjective. (4) cost-effective, ineffective, introspective, irrespective, nonobjective, retrospective.

–ehmp-tiv

(3) pre-emptive, redemptive.

–ip-tiv

(3) descriptive, inscriptive, prescriptive, proscriptive. (4) circumscriptive.

–ehn-tiv

(3) retentive, (4) circumventive, disincentive, inattentive.

–ehp-tiv

(3) conceptive, deceptive, perceptive, receptive. (4) imperceptive.

–ehs-tiv

(2) festive, restive. (3) congestive, digestive, suggestive.

–ik-tiv

(2) fictive. (3) afflictive, conflictive, constrictive, depictive, inflictive, predictive, restrictive, vindictive. (4) contradictive, interdictive.

–ink-tiv

(3) distinctive, instinctive. (4) indistinctive.

–ip-tiv

(3) descriptive, inscriptive, prescriptive, proscriptive. (4) circumscriptive.

–oh-tiv

(2) motive, votive. (3) emotive, promotive. (4) locomotive.

–ohr-tiv

(2) sportive. (3) abortive.

–oo-tiv

(4) attributive, consecutive, constitutive, contributive, diminutive, distributive, executive, persecutive.

–uh-tiv

(3) ablative, additive, amative, causative, cognitive, curative, expletive, fixative, fugitive, genitive, gerundive, hortative, laxative, lenitive, locative, lucrative, narrative, negative, nutritive, optative, positive, primitive, punitive, purgative, relative, sedative, secretive, sensitive, siccative, talkative, tentative, transitive, vocative. (4) abrogative, accusative, acquisitive, adumbrative, affirmative, alternative, appellative, augmentative, comparative, competitive,

conservative, cumulative, declarative, decorative, definitive, demonstrative, derivative, evocative, exhibitive, expectative, explicative, explorative, figurative, imperative, indicative, intuitive, judicative, nominative, operative, palliative, pejorative, preparative, prerogative, preservative, preventative, prohibitive, provocative, remonstrative, repetitive, speculative, superlative. (5) accumulative, alliterative, appreciative, argumentative, associative, commemorative, commiserative, communicative, confederative, cooperative, corroborative, degenerative, deliberative, depreciative, discriminative, exonerative, imaginative, initiative, inoperative, interpretive, interrogative, irradiative, manipulative, recuperative, regenerative, reiterative, representative, vituperative. (6) incommunicative, philoprogenitive.

–uhk-tiv

(3) adductive, conductive, constructive, deductive, destructive, inductive, instructive, obstructive, productive, reductive, seductive. (4) introductive, reproductive, reconstructive.

–uhmp-tiv

(3) assumptive, consumptive, presumptive.

–uhnk-tiv

(3) adjunctive, conjunctive, disjunctive, subjunctive.

–uhp-tiv

(3) corruptive, disruptive.

–uhr-tiv

(2) furtive. (3) assertive, divertive, exertive.

–iz

(1) biz, fizz, friz, his, is, Liz, Ms., quiz, 'tis, viz, whiz, wiz. (2) showbiz.

–izm (–i-zuhm)

(2) chrism, prism, schism. (3) abysm, baptism, Buddhism, Chartism, deism, faddism, Fascism, Jainism, monism, purism, sadism, snobbism, sophism, Sufism, theism, Taoism, truism, Yogism. (4) albinism, altruism, anarchism, aneurysm, Anglicism, animism, aphorism, asterism, atavism, atheism, atomism, Atticism, barbarism, Biblicism, Bolshevism, botulism, Brahmanism, Briticism, brutalism, Byronism, cabalism, Calvinism, cataclysm, catechism, Communism, cretinism, criticism,

cynicism, dandyism, Darwinism, demonism, despotism, dimorphism, ditheism, dogmatism, Druidism, dualism, dynamism, egoism, egotism, embolism, euphemism, exorcism, extremism, fatalism, feminism, fetishism, feudalism, foreignism, formalism, formulism, Gallicism, gigantism, gnosticism, Gothicism, Grundyism, heathenism, Hebraism, hedonism, Hellenism, helotism, heroism, Hinduism, humanism, humorism, hypnotism, jingoism, journalism, Judaism, laconism, lambdacisms, Latinism, legalism, Leninism, localism, magnetism, mannerism, masochism, mechanism, mesmerism, Methodism, modernism, moralism, Mormonism, mysticism, nepotism, nihilism, occultism, organism, optimism, ostracism, pacifism, paganism, pantheism, pauperism, pessimism, pietism, Platonism, pluralism, pragmatism, Quakerism, racialism, realism, rheumatism, Romanism, Satanism, scientism, Semitism, shamanism, skepticism, Socialism, solecism, solipsism, spoonerism, Stalinism, stoicism, syllogism, symbolism, synchronism, syncretism, terrorism, traumatism, tribalism, unionism, vandalism, verbalism, vocalism, volcanism, vulgarism, witticism, Yankeeism, Zionism. (5) absenteeism, absolutism, aestheticism, agnosticism, alcoholism, amateurism, anabolism, anachronism, Anglicanism, antagonism, asceticism, astigmatism, autochthonism, automatism, cannibalism, capitalism, catabolism, Catholicism, charlatanism, collectivism, communalism, Confucianism, conservatism, determinism, diabolism, eclecticism, empiricism, eroticism, evangelism, expressionism, externalism, fanaticism, favoritism, federalism, generalism, hyperbolism, idealism, impressionism, invalidism, Jacobinism, Jesuitism, legitimism, libertinism, literalism, Lutheranism, malapropism, medievalism, mercantilism, metabolism, militarism, monasticism, monotheism, mutualism, nationalism, naturalism, negativism, neologism, objectivism, opportunism, parallelism, paternalism, patriotism, Philistinism, plagiarism, polymorphism, polytheism, positivism, progressivism, Protestantism, provincialism, Puritanism, radicalism, rationalism, recidivism, regionalism, ritualism, romanticism, scholasticism, secessionism, sectionalism, secularism, separatism, somnambulism, subjectivism, syndicalism, universalism, ventriloquism. (6) abolitionism, agrarianism, Americanism, anthropomorphism, Bohemianism, colloquialism, colonialism, conceptualism, conventionalism, cosmopolitanism, equestrianism, evolutionism, existentialism, indeterminism, indifferentism, industrialism, Manicheanism, materialism, Mohammedanism, Occidentalism, Orientalism, parochialism, phenomenalism, postimpressionism, professionalism, Republicanism, Rosicrucianism, sacerdotalism, sectarianism, sensationalism, sentimentalism, spiritualism, traditionalism,

Utopianism, vernacularism. (7) antinomianism, antiquarianism, ceremonialism, Congregationalism, constitutionalism, cosmopolitanism, experimentalism, individualism, intellectualism, internationalism, Presbyterianism, proletarianism, supernaturalism, Unitarianism, vegetarianism, (8) Aristotelianism, humanitarianism, utilitarianism.

–oh

(1) beau, blow, bow, crow, doe, dough, eau, Flo, floe, flow, foe, fro, glow, go, grow, hoe, Jo, Joe, know, lo, low, mot, mow, no, O, oh, owe, Po, pro, rho, roe, row, sew, show, sloe, slow, snow, so, sow, stow, throe, throw, toe, tow, trow, whoa, woe. (2) aglow, ago, although, banjo, below, bestow, bon mot, Bordeaux, bravo, bubo, bureau, chapeau, château, Chi-Rho, cockcrow, cocoa, dado, depot, dido, Dido, duo, euro, forego, foreknow, foreshow, Frisco, gecko, heigh-ho, hello, jabot, Jane Doe, John Doe, Juno, Keogh, KO, Leo, macho, merlot, Miró, Monroe, moonglow, no-show, nouveau, oboe, outgrow, Pluto, poncho, quarto, rainbow, sabot, tableau, tiptoe, toro, trousseau, Van Gogh, Virgo. (3) afterglow, al fresco, allegro, apropos, art nouveau, buffalo, Buffalo, bungalow, calico, cameo, Cicero, domino, embryo, Eskimo, falsetto, Figaro, folio, furbelow, gazebo, gigolo, HMO, Iago, Idaho, indigo, Mario, memento, Mexico, mistletoe, mulatto, Navajo, nuncio, octavo, Ohio, oleo, overflow, overgrow, overthrow, portico, portmanteau, potato, Prospero, radio, Romeo, Scorpio, sloppy joe, so-and-so, sourdough, staccato, stiletto, studio, tae kwon do, tallyho, tobacco, Tókyo, tomato, torero, torpedo, tremolo, ultimo, undergo, undertow, vertigo, video, vireo, volcano. (4) Acapulco, a capriccio, adagio, bravissimo, fortissimo, imbroglio, incognito, intaglio, magnifico, malapropos, mustachio, Ontario, oregano, pistachio, politico, seraglio. (5) accelerando, archipelago, braggadocio, duodecimo, impresario, oratorio, pianissimo. (6) generalissimo.

–ee-oh

(2) Cleo, Leo, Rio, trio. (3) Borneo, folio, olio, polio, radio, rodeo, stereo. (4) portfolio.

–ehr-oh

(2) arrow, barrow, faro, harrow, marrow, narrow, pharaoh, sparrow, tarot, yarrow. (3) bolero, dinero, sombrero, torero. (4) caballero. (5) banderillero, embarcadero.

–ir-oh

(2) hero, Nero, zero.

–ohr-oh

(2) borrow, morrow, sorrow. (3) tomorrow.

–uhr-oh

(2) borough, burro, burrow, furrow, thorough.

–aam-boh

(2) ambo, crambo, flambeau, sambo.

–im-boh

(2) bimbo, limbo. (3) akimbo.

–ee-boh

(2) gazebo, placebo.

–oh-boh

(2) hobo, lobo, oboe.

–uhm-boh

(2) Dumbo, gumbo, jumbo. (4) mumbo-jumbo.

–ah-doh

(3) bravado, Mikado. (4) avocado, Colorado, desperado, El Dorado.
(5) amontillado (6) aficionado. (7) incommunicado.

–ay-doh

(2) dado. (3) tornado.

–ee-doh

(2) credo, Lido. (3) libido, Toledo, torpedo, tuxedo.

–oh-doh

(2) dodo, Fodo. (3) Quasimodo.

–oo-doh

(2) judo, kudo, pseudo. (3) escudo, Menudo, testudo.

–aang-goh

(2) mango, tango. (3) fandango.

–ah-goh

(3) Chicago. (4) Asiago, Santiago.

–ahng-**goh** (–awng-**goh**)

(2) bongo, Congo.

–ahr-**goh**

(2) argot, cargo, Fargo, largo, Margot. (3) embargo, Wells Fargo.
(4) supercargo.

–ay-**goh**

(2) sago. (3) farrago, imago, lumbago, virago.

–ing-**goh**

(2) bingo, dingo, gringo, jingo, lingo. (3) Domingo, flamingo.

–eh-**koh**

(2) echo, Eco, gecko, secco. (3) art deco, El Greco.

–oh-**koh**

(2) coco, cocoa, loco, Yoko. (3) rococo. (4) Orinoco.

–aa-**loh**

(2) aloe, callow, fallow, mallow, sallow, shallow, tallow.

–ah-**loh**

(2) follow, hollow, Rollo, swallow, wallow. (3) Apollo.

–eh-**loh**

(2) bellow, cello, felloe, fellow, hello, Jello, mellow, yellow.
(3) bedfellow, bordello, duello, good fellow, Longfellow,
marshmallow, Othello. (4) Donatello, Monticello, Punchinello,
saltarello.

–i-**loh**

(2) billow, pillow, willow. (3) Negrillo. (4) armadillo, cigarillo,
peccadillo, Tiparillo.

–oh-**loh**

(2) bolo, polo, solo. (4) Marco Polo, water polo.

–oh-**moh**

(2) chromo, Como, homo, promo. (3) majordomo.

–ee-**noh**

(2) keno, Reno, Zeno. (3) bambino, casino, merino. (4) Filipino,
maraschino.

–ei-noh

(2) lino, rhino. (3) albino.

–i-noh

(2) minnow, winnow.

–ei-roh

(2) Cairo, Chi Ro, giro, gyro, tyro. (2) autogiro.

–oo-soh

(2) Crusoe, trousseau, whoso. (3) Caruso.

–aa-toh

(2) chateau, plateau.

–aan-toh

(2) canto. (3) portmanteau.

–ah-toh

(2) blotto, grotto, lotto, motto, Otto. (3) legato, mulatto, potato, tomato, staccato. (4) obbligato, pizzicato. (5) inamorato.

–ay-toh

(2) Cato, NATO, Plato. (3) potato, tomato.

–ee-toh

(2) Tito, veto. (3) bonito, mosquito. (4) Hirohito, incognito.

–eh-toh

(2) ghetto. (3) falsetto, Geppetto, in petto, libretto, palmetto, stiletto, zucchetto. (4) allegretto, lazaretto, Rigoletto, Tintoretto.

–ehn-toh

(2) cento, lento. (3) memento, pimento. (4) Sacramento, divertimento.

–ehs-toh

(2) pesto, presto. (4) manifesto.

–in-toh

(2) pinto, Shinto.

–oh-toh

(2) photo, Toto. (3) De Soto, Kyoto.

–ohb

(1) daub, globe, Job, lobe, probe, robe, strobe. (2) conglobe, disrobe, enrobe, microbe. (3) Anglophobe, Francophobe, homophobe, xenophobe.

–ohch

(1) broach, brooch, coach, loach, poach, roach. (2) approach, cockroach, encroach, reproach.

–ohd

(1) bode, code, goad, hoed, load, lode, mode, node, ode, road, rode, strode, toad. (2) abode, anode, cathode, commode, corrode, erode, explode, forebode, geode, implode, payload, railroad, reload, unload, zip code. (3) à la mode, discommode, episode, overload, pigeon-toed. (4) area code.
ALSO: –oh + -ed (i.e., *snowed*, *tiptoed*).

–ohf

(1) loaf, oaf. (2) meatloaf, sugarloaf.

–ohg

(1) brogue, rogue, vogue. (2) pirogue, prorogue. (3) disembogue.

–ohk

(1) bloke, broke, choke, cloak, coke, Coke, croak, folk, joke, oak, poke, smoke, soak, spoke, stoke, stroke, toke, toque, woke, yoke, yolk. (2) awoke, backstroke, baroque, bespoke, convoke, evoke, invoke, kinfolk, provoke, revoke. (3) artichoke, counterstroke, gentlefolk, masterstroke, Roanoke.

–ohks

(1) coax, hoax.
ALSO: –ohk + -s (i.e., *spokes*, *evokes*).

–ohl

(1) bole, boll, bowl, coal, dole, droll, foal, goal, hole, Joel, knoll, kohl, mole, pole, poll, role, roll, scroll, shoal, Sol, sole, soul, stole, stroll, toll, troll, whole. (2) atoll, bankroll, cajole, condole, console, control, Creole, enroll, flagpole, loophole, Maypole, Nicole, parole, patrol, payroll, peephole, petrol. (3) buttonhole, camisole, girandole, oriole, rigmarole, rock 'n' roll, Seminole.

–ohld

(1) bold, cold, doled, fold, gold, hold, mold, mould, old, scold, sold, told, wold. (2) behold, blindfold, cuckold, enfold, foothold, foretold, freehold, household, retold, stronghold, threshold, toehold, twofold, unfold, untold, uphold, withhold. (3) centerfold, manifold, marigold, overbold. ALSO: **–ohl** + *-ed* (i.e., *scrolled, enrolled*).

–ohlt

(1) bolt, colt, dolt, jolt, molt, poult, volt. (2) revolt, unbolt. (3) thunderbolt.

–ohm

(1) chrome, comb, dome, foam, gnome, home, loam, Nome, ohm, Om, roam, Rome, tome. (2) cockscomb, coulomb, Jerome, syndrome. (3) aerodrome, catacomb, currycomb, gastronome, hippodrome, honeycomb, metronome, monochrome, palindrome, ribosome, Styrofoam.

–ohn

(1) bone, cone, crone, drone, groan, hone, Joan, loan, lone, moan, own, phone, pone, prone, roan, Rhone, scone, shone, stone, throne, tone, zone. (2) alone, atone, backbone, Bayonne, bemoan, brimstone, cell phone, cologne, condone, curbstone, dethrone, disown, enthrone, flagstone, foreshown, grindstone, headstone, intone, keystone, milestone, millstone, moonstone, ozone, postpone, tombstone, trombone, unknown. (3) baritone, chaperone, cicerone, cornerstone, gramophone, megaphone, microphone, monotone, overgrown, saxophone, speakerphone, telephone, undertone, xylophone. (4) progesterone, testosterone. ALSO: **–oh** + *-n* (i.e., *shown, overthrown*).

–ohp

(1) cope, dope, grope, hope, lope, mope, nope, pope, rope, scope, slope, soap, taupe, trope. (2) elope. (3) antelope, antipope, cantaloupe, envelope, gyroscope, horoscope, interlope, isotope, microscope, misanthrope, periscope, stethoscope, telescope, zoetrope. (4) heliotrope, kaleidoscope.

–ohr

(1) boar, Boer, bore, chore, corps, door, floor, for, four, gore, hoar, lore, more, nor, oar, o'er, or, ore, pore, pour, roar, score, shore, snore, soar, sore, store, swore, Thor, tore, whore, war, wore, yore, your. (2) abhor, adore, afore, ashore, before, claymore, deplore, encore, explore, folklore, footsore, forbore, forswore, galore, ignore, implore, rapport, restore, senior. (3) albacore, battledore, Baltimore, carnivore, commodore, corridor, cuspidor, dinosaur, Ecuador, evermore, furthermore, hellebore, herbivore, heretofore, Labrador, matador, metaphor, meteor, Minotaur, nevermore, omnivore, petit four, pinafore, piscivore, Salvador, semaphore, Singapore, sophomore, sycamore, troubadour, underscore. (4) ichthyosaur, toreador, tyrannosaur.

–ehn-tohr

(2) centaur, mentor, stentor.

–ohrb

(1) orb. (2) absorb.

–ohrch

(1) porch, scorch, torch.

–ohrd

(1) board, chord, cord, fjord, ford, Ford, gourd, hoard, horde, lord, sword, toward. (2) aboard, accord, afford, award, broadsword, concord, discord, landlord, record, reward, seaboard, untoward, warlord. (3) clavichord, harpsichord, mortarboard, smorgasbord, storyboard. ALSO: **–ohr** + -ed (i.e., *warred, restored*).

–ee-bohrd

(2) keyboard, seaboard.

–ohrf

(1) dwarf, Orff, morph, wharf. (3) endomorph, mesomorph.

–ohrj

(1) forge, George, gorge. (2) disgorge, engorge.

–ohrk

(1) cork, fork, pork, stork, torque, York. (2) bulwark, New York, pitchfork, uncork.

–ohrm

(1) corm, dorm, form, norm, storm, swarm, warm. (2) brainstorm, conform, deform, freeform, hailstorm, inform, perform, rainstorm, reform, snowstorm, transform. (3) chloroform, cruciform, misinform, multiform, thunderstorm, uniform, vermiform. (4) cuneiform.

–ohrn

(1) born, borne, bourn, corn, horn, morn, mourn, scorn, shorn, sworn, thorn, torn, warn, worn. (2) acorn, adorn, blackthorn, buckthorn, firstborn, foghorn, forewarn, forlorn, forsworn, greenhorn, hawthorn, lovelorn, outworn, popcorn, stillborn, suborn, unborn. (3) alpenhorn, barleycorn, Capricorn, Matterhorn, peppercorn, unicorn.

–ohrp

(1) thorp, warp.

–ohrs

(1) coarse, course, force, gorse, hoarse, horse, Morse, Norse, source. (2) concourse, discourse, divorce, endorse, enforce, main course, perforce, recourse, remorse, resource, seahorse, unhorse. (3) hobbyhorse, intercourse, reinforce, watercourse.

–ohrt

(1) court, fort, forte, mort, ort, port, quart, short, snort, sort, sport, swart, thwart, tort, torte, wart, wort. (2) abort, airport, assort, athwart, cavort, cohort, comport, consort, contort, deport, disport, distort, escort, exhort, export, extort, import, Newport, passport, purport, report, resort, retort, seaport, Shreveport, transport. (3) Saint John's wort.

–ohrthh

(1) forth, fourth, north. (2) henceforth, thenceforth.

–ohrts

(1) quartz.
ALSO: **–ohrt** + -s (i.e., *sports*, *exhorts*).

–ohrz

(1) yours.
ALSO: **–ohr** + -s (i.e., *soars*, *abhors*).

–ohs

(1) close, dose, gross. (2) cosmos, dextrose, engross, Eros, fructose, glucose, jocose, lactose, morose, verbose. (3) adios, adipose, bellicose, cellulose, comatose, diagnose, grandiose, lachrymose, otiose, overdose.

–ohst

(1) boast, coast, ghost, grossed, host, most, post, roast, toast.
(2) almost, East Coast, engrossed, Gold Coast, foremost, hindmost, riposte, seacoast, signpost, West Coast. (3) aftermost, diagnosed, furthermost, hindermost, hitching post, nethermost, outermost, over-dosed, undermost, uppermost, uttermost.

–oht

(1) bloat, boat, Choate, coat, cote, dote, float, gloat, goat, moat, mote, note, oat, quote, rote, shoat, smote, stoat, throat, tote, vote, wrote.
(2) afloat, catboat, compote, connote, coyote, demote, denote, devote, emote, footnote, keynote, lifeboat, misquote, outvote, promote, remote, steamboat, topcoat, tugboat, unquote. (3) anecdote, antidote, asymptote, billy goat, creosote, nanny goat, overcoat, petticoat, redingote, riverboat, sugarcoat.

–ohth

(1) clothe, loathe. (2) betroth.

–ohthh

(1) both, growth, loath, oath. (3) overgrowth, undergrowth.

–ohv

(1) clove, cove, dove, drove, grove, hove, Jove, mauve, rove, shrove, stove, strove, throve, trove, wove. (2) alcove, by Jove, mangrove. (3) interwove, treasure trove.

–oo

(1) blew, blue, boo, brew, chew, clue, coo, coup, crew, cue, dew, do, drew, due, ewe, few, flew, flu, flue, glue, gnu, goo, grew, hew, Hugh, Jew, knew, lieu, loo, Lou, mew, moo, mu, new, pew, phew, queue, rue, screw, shoe, shrew, skew, slew, slough, sous, spew, stew, strew, sue, Sue, threw, through, to, too, true, two, view, who, woo, yew, you, zoo.
(2) accrue, adieu, ado, ague, Andrew, anew, askew, bamboo, bedew, bijou, cachou, canoe, cashew, cuckoo, curfew, curlew, debut, drive-through, emu, endue, ensue, eschew, Hindu, imbue, issue, juju, Kung fu, menu, mildew, milieu, Peru, pooh-pooh, pursue, purview, ragout,

renew, review, shampoo, subdue, taboo, tattoo, tissue, tutu, undo, venue, voodoo, withdrew, yahoo, yoo-hoo, Zulu. (3) avenue, barbeque, billet-doux, cockatoo, curlicue, déjà vu, interview, kangaroo, misconstrue, residue, retinue, revenue, Timbuktu. (4) Kalamazoo, merci beaucoup.

–oo-loo

(2) Lulu, Zulu. (3) Honolulu.

–uhr-loo

(2) curlew, purlieu.

–ehn-yoo

(2) menu, venue.

–ehsk-yoo

(2) fescue, rescue.

–in-yoo

(2) sinew. (3) continue, retinue. (4) discontinue.

–ish-yoo

(2) issue, tissue. (3) reissue.

–oob

(1) boob, cube, rube, Rube, tube. (2) boob tube, ice cube (3) inner tube.

–ood

(1) brood, cued, crude, dude, feud, food, Jude, lewd, mood, nude, prude, rood, rude, shrewd, snood, who'd, you'd. (2) collude, conclude, delude, denude, elude, etude, exclude, extrude, exude, include, intrude, obtrude, occlude, preclude, prelude, protrude, seclude. (3) Altitude, amplitude, aptitude, attitude, certitude, desuetude, fortitude, gratitude, habitude, interlude, lassitude, latitude, longitude, magnitude, multitude, platitude, plentitude, promptitude, pulchritude, quietude, rectitude, servitude, solitude, turpitude. (4) Beatitude, exactitude, ingratitude, necessitude, similitude, solicitude, vicissitude. (6) Verisimilitude.
ALSO: –oo + -ed (i.e., glued, mildewed).

–oof

(1) Goof, pouf, proof, roof, spoof. (2) Aloof, disproof, fireproof, fool-proof, rainproof, reproof, Tartuffe. (3) Waterproof, weatherproof.

–ooj

(1) huge, Scrooge, stooge. (2) deluge, refuge. (3) centrifuge, febrifuge, subterfuge.

–ook

(1) cuke, duke, fluke, juke, kook, Luke, nuke, puke, spook, uke.
(2) archduke, Baruch, rebuke. (3) Marmaduke, Pentateuch.

–ool

(1) cool, drool, fool, fuel, ghoul, mewl, mule, pool, rule, school, spool, stool, tool, tulle, who'll, you'll, Yule. (2) ampoule, befool, footstool, home rule, misrule, toadstool, whirlpool. (3) Golden Rule, Liverpool, molecule, overrule, reticule, ridicule, vestibule.

–ahd-yool

(2) module, nodule.

–oom

(1) bloom, boom, broom, brume, doom, flume, fume, gloom, groom, loom, plume, rheum, room, spume, tomb, whom, womb, zoom. (2) abloom, assume, bathroom, bedroom, bridegroom, consume, entomb, exhume, heirloom, illume, Khartoum, legume, perfume, resume, simoom, subsume, vacuum. (3) anteroom, elbowroom, va-va-voom.

–oon

(1) boon, Boone, coon, croon, dune, goon, hewn, June, loon, moon, noon, prune, rune, soon, spoon, strewn, swoon, toon, tune. (2) attune, baboon, balloon, bassoon, bestrewn, buffoon, cartoon, cocoon, commune, doubloon, dragoon, festoon, forenoon, galloon, harpoon, high noon, immune, impugn, jejune, lagoon, lampoon, maroon, monsoon, Neptune, oppugn, platoon, poltroon, pontoon, quadroon, raccoon, Rangoon, spittoon, tycoon, typhoon, Walloon. (3) afternoon, Brigadoon, Cameroon, honeymoon, importune, macaroon, octoroon, opportune, pantaloon, picaroon, picayune.

–oond

(1) wound.
ALSO: **–oon** + -ed (i.e., *swooned*, *honeymooned*).

–oop

(1) coop, croup, droop, drupe, dupe, goop, group, hoop, loop, poop, scoop, shoop, sloop, soup, stoop, stoup, swoop, troop, troupe, whoop. (2) recoup. (3) Guadeloupe, nincompoop.

–oos

(1) Bruce, deuce, goose, juice, loose, moose, mousse, noose, puce, sluice, spruce, truce, use, Zeus. (2) abstruse, abuse, adduce, burnoose, caboose, conduce, couscous, deduce, diffuse, disuse, excuse, induce, misuse, mongoose, obtuse, papoose, produce, profuse, recluse, reduce, seduce, Toulouse, traduce, vamoose. (3) calaboose, introduce, reproduce, Syracuse. (4) hypotenuse.

–oosh

(1) douche, ruche, whoosh. (2) barouche, cartouche, debouch.
(3) scaramouch.

–oost

(1) boost, Proust, roost.
ALSO: **–oos** + *-ed* (i.e., *juiced*, *introduced*).

–oot

(1) beaut, boot, brute, butte, chute, coot, cute, flute, fruit, hoot, jute, loot, lute, moot, mute, newt, root, route, scoot, shoot, suit, toot. (2) acute, Aleut, astute, Beirut, breadfruit, cahoots, cheroot, commute, compute, confute, crapshoot, depute, dilute, dispute, hirsute, impute, minute, pollute, pursuit, recruit, refute, salute, transmute, uproot, volute. (3) absolute, attribute, bandicoot, bodysuit, constitute, destitute, disrepute, dissolute, execute, institute, kiwifruit, malamute, overshoot, parachute, persecute, prosecute, prostitute, resolute, substitute. (4) electrocute, irresolute, reconstitute.

–ooth

(1) smooth, soothe.

–oothh

(1) booth, couth, Ruth, sleuth, sooth, tooth, truth, youth. (2) Duluth, forsooth, uncouth, vermouth.

–oov

(1) groove, Louvre, move, prove, who've, you've. (2) approve, behoove, disprove, improve, remove, reprove. (3) disapprove.

–ooz

(1) booze, bruise, cruise, fuse, muse, news, ooze, ruse, snooze, use, who's, whose. (2) abuse, accuse, amuse, bemuse, confuse, diffuse, disuse, enthuse, excuse, infuse, misuse, peruse, recuse, refuse, suffuse, transfuse. (3) disabuse, Syracuse.

ALSO: **–oo** + *-s* (i.e., *blues, tattoos*).

–ow

(1) bough, bow, brow, chow, ciao, cow, dhow, Dow, frau, how, now, plough, plow, prow, row, scow, slough, sow, Tao, thou, trow, vow, wow. (2) allow, avow, bow-wow, endow, highbrow, hoosegow, know-how, kowtow, landau, lowbrow, meow, Moscow, powwow, snowplow, somehow. (3) anyhow, disallow, disavow, middlebrow.

–owch

(1) couch, crouch, grouch, ouch, pouch, slouch, vouch. (2) avouch.

–owd

(1) cloud, crowd, loud, proud, shroud. (2) aloud, enshroud, overcrowd. (3) thundercloud.

ALSO: **–ow** + *-ed* (i.e., *vowed, disallowed*).

–owl

(1) cowl, foul, fowl, growl, howl, jowl, owl, prowl, scowl, yowl. (2) afoul, befoul. (3) waterfowl.

–own

(1) brown, clown, crown, down, drown, frown, gown, noun, town. (2) adown, boomtown, Cape Town, downtown, embrown, Georgetown, Jamestown, nightgown, pronoun, renown, uptown. (3) Allentown, button-down, Chinatown, eiderdown, hand-me-down, shantytown, upside down, watered-down.

–ownd

(1) bound, found, ground, hound, mound, pound, round, sound, wound. (2) abound, aground, around, astound, background, bloodhound, compound, confound, dumbfound, expound, hidebound, inbound, outbound, profound, propound, rebound, redound, renowned, resound, spellbound, snowbound, surround, unbound, unfound. (3) ultrasound, underground, wraparound. (4) merry-go-round.

ALSO: **–own** + *-ed* (i.e., *browned, frowned*)

–owns

(1) bounce, flounce, jounce, ounce, pounce, trounce. (2) announce, denounce, enounce, pronounce, renounce.
ALSO: **–ownt** + -s (i.e., *mounts*, *accounts*).

–ownt

(1) count, fount, mount. (2) account, amount, dismount, recount, remount, surmount. (3) catamount, paramount, tantamount.

–is-kownt

(2) discount, miscount, viscount.

–owr

SEE: **–ow-uhr**.

–ows

(1) blouse, douse, dowse, grouse, house, louse, mouse, souse, spouse, Strauss. (2) backhouse, birdhouse, clubhouse, delouse, doghouse, espouse, hothouse, outhouse, penthouse, poorhouse, roundhouse, storehouse, warehouse. (3) Mickey Mouse, Mighty Mouse, powerhouse, summerhouse.

–owst

(1) doused, Faust, joust, oust, soused. (2) deloused.

–owt

(1) bout, clout, doubt, drought, flout, gout, grout, knout, kraut, lout, out, pout, rout, scout, shout, snout, spout, sprout, stout, tout, trout. (2) ablaut, about, blackout, brownout, devout, lookout, redoubt, takeout, throughout, umlaut, whiteout, without. (3) gadabout, hereabout, knockabout, out-and-out, roundabout, roustabout, sauerkraut, thereabout, waterspout.

–owth

(1) mouth, south.

–owz

(1) browse, douse, dowse, house, rouse. (2) arouse, carouse, espouse.
ALSO: **–ow** + -s (i.e., *boughs*, *disavows*).

–oy

(1) boy, buoy, cloy, coy, goy, joy, oy, ploy, poi, Roy, soy, toy, troy, Troy. (2) ahoy, alloy, annoy, batboy, busboy, choirboy, convoy, decoy, deploy, enjoy, employ, envoy, Leroy, McCoy, Rob Roy, Saint Croix, Savoy, viceroy. (3) corduroy, Illinois, Iroquois, misemploy.

–ow-boy

(2) cowboy, ploughboy.

–oyd

(1) Floyd, Freud, Lloyd, void. (2) ovoid, steroid, tabloid. (3) alkaloid, aneroid, asteroid, celluloid, Mongoloid, Polaroid, trapezoid.
ALSO: –oy + -ed (i.e., *cloyed*, *enjoyed*).

–oyl

(1) boil, broil, coil, Doyle, foil, moil, oil, roil, soil, spoil, toil.
(2) despoil, embroil, gumboil, parboil, recoil, tinfoil, trefoil, turmoil, uncoil. (3) hydrofoil, quatrefoil.

–oyn

(1) coin, groin, join, loin, quoin. (2) adjoin, conjoin, Des Moines, disjoin, enjoin, purloin, rejoin, sirloin, subjoin. (3) tenderloin.

–oynt

(1) joint, point. (2) anoint, appoint, ballpoint, conjoint, disjoint, drypoint, West Point. (3) counterpoint, disappoint, needlepoint, petit point.

–oys

(1) choice, Joyce, voice. (2) invoice, rejoice, Rolls Royce.

–oyst

(1) foist, hoist, joist, moist, voiced. (2) invoiced, rejoiced.

–oyt

(1) doit, quoit. (2) adroit, Beloit, Detroit, exploit, introit. (3) maladroit.

–oyz

(1) noise, poise. (2) turquoise. (3) counterpoise, equipoise, Tinkertoys.
ALSO: –oy + -s (i.e., *joys*, *corduroys*).

–ohz

(1) chose, close, clothes, doze, froze, gloze, hose, nose, pose, prose, rose, Rose, those. (2) ambrose, arose, compose, depose, disclose, dispose, enclose, expose, foreclose, impose, oppose, propose, repose, suppose, transpose, tuberose, unclose, unfroze. (3) decompose, discompose, indispose, interpose, predispose, presuppose. (4) metamorphose, superimpose.

ALSO: **–oh** + -*s* (i.e., *knows*, *zeros*.)

–uh

(1) ah, baa, bah, blah, bra, ha, la, ma, pa, pas, Ra, shah, spa. (2) a-ha, Bourgeois, cha cha, éclat, état, faux pas, grandma, grandpa, ha-ha, hurrah, huzza, Libra, mama, papa, pasha, Shiva, Vesta, viva, voilà. (3) angora, baccarat, coup d'état, Mardi Gras, nebula, Omaha, Ottawa, panama, Panama, Shangri-la. (4) Ali Baba, ayatollah, utopia. (5) hypochondria, pyromania.

–ee-uh

(2) Leah, Mia. (3) Althea, chorea, Crimea, idea, Judea, Korea, Maria, Medea, obeah, Sofia, spirea, tortilla. (4) Caesarea, diarrhea, gonorrhea, panacea, pizzeria, Tanzania. (5) Cassiopeia, pharmacopoeia. (6) onomatopoeia.

–ehr-uh

(2) Clara, era, Hera, Sarah, Tara. (3) chimera, mascara, tiara.

–ir-uh

(2) era, lira, Vera. (3) Madeira, chimera.

–oh-uh

(2) boa, moa, Noah, proa. (3) aloha, Genoa, jerboa. (4) Samoa. (5) Krakatoa, protozoa, Shenandoah.

–ohr-uh

(2) aura, Cora, Dora, flora, Flora, hora, Laura, mora, Norah, Torah. (3) angora, Aurora, fedora, Marmora, menorah, Pandora, signora.

–uur-uh

(2) pleura. (3) bavura, caesura. (4) coloratura. (5) appoggiatura.

–oo-buh

(2) Cuba, juba, scuba, tuba. (3) Aruba.

–ah-**bruh**

(2) sabra. (4) candelabra.

–aan-**duh**

(2) panda. (3) Amanda, Miranda, veranda. (4) jacaranda, memoranda, propaganda.

–ah-**duh**

(2) Dada. (3) armada, cicada, Grenada, Nevada. (4) enchilada.
(6) Sierra Nevada.

–ehn-**duh**

(2) Brenda, Glenda, Zenda. (3) addenda, agenda, credenda.
(4) corrigenda, hacienda.

–oh-**duh**

(2) coda, Rhoda, soda, Yoda. (3) Baroda, pagoda.

–oh-**guh**

(2) toga, yoga. (3) Saratoga. (5) Ticonderoga.

–eh-**kuh**

(2) Mecca. (3) Rebecca.

–ei-**kuh**

(2) mica, Micah, pica. (3) Formica.

–eh-**luh**

(2) Bella, Ella, fella, Stella. (3) cappella, Louella, patella, umbrella.
(4) Cinderella, Isabella, tarantella.

–i-**luh**

(2) Scylla, villa, Willa. (3) ancilla, Attila, axilla, Camilla, cedilla, chinchilla, flotilla, gorilla, guerilla, manila, Manila, mantilla, maxilla, megillah, Priscilla, vanilla. (4) camarilla, cascarilla, sabadilla.
(5) sarsaparilla.

–oh-**luh**

(2) cola, kola, Lola, Nola, Zola. (3) Angola, canola, gondola, granola, payola, viola. (4) ayatollah, Espanola, gladiola, Gorgonzola, Hispaniola, Pensacola.

–oo-**luh**

(2) Beulah, hula, moola. (3) Tallulah. (4) Ashtabula.

–ah-muh

(2) Brahma, comma, drama, lama, llama, mama, Rama. (3) pajama. (4) Dalai Lama, diorama, docudrama, Fujiyama, georama, melodrama, panorama.

–eh-muh

(2) Emma, gemma. (3) dilemma.

–ig-muh

(2) sigma, stigma. (3) enigma.

–oh-muh

(2) coma, Roma, soma. (3) aroma, diploma, sarcoma, Tacoma. (4) carcinoma, Oklahoma.

–oo-muh

(2) duma, puma, summa, Uma, Yuma. (4) Montezuma.

–uhr-muh

(2) Burma, derma, Erma, Irma. (4) terra firma.

–aa-nuh

(2) Anna, Hannah, Jana, manna. (3) banana, bandana, cabana, Diana, Havana, hosanna, Montana, savannah, Savannah, sultana, Urbana. (4) Indiana, Juliana, Pollyanna, Susquehanna. (5) Louisiana.

–ah-nuh

(2) Anna, Ghana. (3) Botswana, gymkhana, iguana, nirvana, piranha, sultana. (4) marijuana, Tatiana, Tijuana.

–ee-nuh

(2) Dina, Gina, Lena, Nina, Tina. (3) arena, Athena, cantina, catena, Christina, czarina, Edwina, farina, galena, Georgina, Helena, hyena, Katrina, marina, Medina, Messina, patina, Regina, retsina, Rowena, subpoena, tsarina, verbena. (4) Angelina, ballerina, Catalina, cavatina, concertina, ocarina, Pasadena, scarlatina, semolina, signorina, Wilhelmina.

–eh-nuh

(2) henna, senna. (3) antenna, duenna, Ravenna, Siena, sienna, Vienna.

–ei-nuh

(2) china, China, Dinah, Ina, myna. (4) Carolina.

–oo-nuh

(2) luna, puna, tuna. (3) kahuna, lacuna, Laguna, vicuna.

–ei-ruh

(2) Ira, Myra. (3) Elmira, Elvira, hegira, Palmyra.

–oh-suh

(3) Formosa, mimosa, samosa. (4) Mariposa, vituosa.

–uh-shuh

(2) Prussia, Russia.

–aa-tuh

(2) data, strata. (3) pro rata.

–aan-tuh

(2) Santa. (3) Atlanta, infanta, Vedanta. (4) Atalanta.

–ah-tuh

(3) cantata, errata, frittata, piñata, regatta, sonata, toccata,
(4) caponata, serenata, terra cotta.

–ay-tuh

(2) beta, data, eta, theta, zeta. (3) errata, pro rata. (4) ultimata,
vertebrata.

–ee-tuh

(2) cheetah, pita, Rita, vita. (3) Anita, Juanita, Lolita, partita.
(4) incognita, margarita, Margarita, señorita.

–ehn-tuh

(2) yenta. (3) magenta, placenta, polenta. (5) impedimenta.

–ehs-tuh

(2) Vesta. (3) celesta, fiesta, siesta.

–oh-tuh

(2) quota, rota. (3) Dakota, iota, Lakota. (4) Minnesota.

–ah-vuh

(2) brava, fava, guava, Java, lava. (3) cassava. (4) balaclava.

–oh-vuh

(2) nova, ova. (3) Jehovah. (4) Casanova, supernova, Villanova.

–aan-zuh

(2) stanza. (3) bonanza, organza. (5) extravaganza.

–ah-zuh

(2) Gaza, plaza. (3) piazza.

–ehn-zuh

(2) cadenza, credenza, influenza.

–oo-zuh

(2) Sousa. (3) medusa, mezuzah. (5) lollapalooza.

–uhb

(1) bub, chub, club, cub, drub, dub, grub, hub, nub, pub, rub, scrub, shrub, snub, stub, sub, tub. (2) hubbub. (3) rub-a-dub. (4) Beelzebub.

–aa-ruhb

(2) Arab, carob, scarab.

–uhch

(1) clutch, crutch, Dutch, hutch, much, smutch, such, touch. (2) retouch. (3) double Dutch, inasmuch, insomuch, overmuch.

–uhd

(1) blood, bud, cud, dud, flood, mud, scud, spud, stud, thud.
(2) lifeblood, rosebud, scud stud.

–uhf

(1) bluff, buff, chough, chuff, cuff, duff, fluff, gruff, guff, huff, muff, puff, rough, ruff, scruff, scuff, slough, snuff, sough, stuff, tough, tuff.
(2) breadstuff, earmuff, enough, rebuff. (3) huff-and-puff, overstuff, powder puff.

–uhg

(1) bug, chug, drug, dug, hug, jug, lug, mug, plug, pug, rug, shrug, slug, smug, snug, thug, tug. (2) humbug. (3) doodlebug, jitterbug, litterbug.

–uhj

(1) budge, drudge, fudge, grudge, judge, nudge, sludge, smudge, trudge.
(2) adjudge, begrudge, forejudge, misjudge, prejudge.

–uhk

(1) buck, chuck, Chuck, cluck, duck, luck, muck, pluck, puck, Puck, schmuck, shuck, snuck, struck, stuck, suck, truck, tuck. (2) amok, amuck, awestruck, dumbstruck, moonstruck, potluck, roebuck, starstruck, woodchuck. (3) thunderstruck, nip-and-tuck, sitting duck, wonderstruck.

–uh-muhk

(2) hummock, stomach.

–uhks

(1) crux, flux, lux, tux. (2) conflux, efflux, influx, reflux.
ALSO: **–uhk** + -s (i.e., *trucks*, *woodchucks*).

–uhkt

(1) duct. (2) abduct, conduct, induct, instruct, obstruct. (3) aqueduct, misconduct, oviduct, usufruct, viaduct.
ALSO: **–uhk** + -ed (i.e., *bucked*, *plucked*)

–uhl

(1) cull, dull, gull, hull, lull, mull, null, scull, skull. (2) annul, numskull, seagull.

–aan-yoo-uhl

(2) annual, manual. (3) Emmanuel.

–ee-nee-uhl

(2) genial, menial, venial. (3) congenial.

–ehr-uhl

(2) barrel, beryl, carol, Carole, carrel, Cheryl, feral, ferule, ferrule, Merrill, Meryl, peril, sterile. (3) apparel.

–ei-uhl

(2) dial, phial, trial, vial, viol. (3) decrial, denial, espial, mistrial, retrial, sundial.

–ohr-uhl

(2) aural, chloral, choral, coral, floral, horal, laurel, moral, oral, quarrel, sorrel. (3) auroral, immoral, sororal.

–oo-uhl

(2) crewel, cruel, dual, duel, fuel, gruel, jewel, newel. (3) accrual, bejewel, eschewal, refuel, renewal.

–ow-uhl

(2) bowel, dowel, rowel, towel, trowel, vowel. (3) avowal.
(4) disembowel.

–oy-uhl

(2) loyal, royal. (3) disloyal.

–uur-uhl

(2) crural, jural, mural, neural, pleural, plural, rural, Ural. (4) intramural.

–aa-buhl

(2) babble, dabble, drabble, gabble, grabble, rabble, scrabble.
(3) hardscrabble.

–aam-buhl

(2) amble, bramble, Campbell, gamble, gambol, ramble, scramble, shamble. (3) preamble.

–ah-buhl

(2) cobble, gobble, hobble, nobble, squabble, wobble.

–ahr-buhl

(2) barbel, garble, marble.

–ay-buhl

(2) Abel, able, cable, fable, gable, label, Mabel, sable, stable, table.
(3) Disable, enable, timetable, unable, unstable.

–eh-buhl

(2) pebble, rebel, treble.

–ehm-buhl

(2) tremble. (3) assemble, dissemble. (4) disassemble, reassemble.

–ei-buhl

(2) bible, Bible, libel, tribal.

–i-buhl

(2) dibble, dribble, kibble, nibble, quibble, scribble, sybil, Sybil.

–im-buhl

(2) cymbal, gimbal, nimble, symbol, thimble, tymbal, wimble.

–ohr-buhl

(2) corbel, warble.

–uh-buhl

(2) bubble, double, Hubble, rubble, stubble, trouble.

–uhm-buhl

(2) bumble, crumble, fumble, grumble, humble, jumble, mumble, rumble, scumble, stumble, tumble, umbel.

–ehs-chuhl

(2) bestial. (3) celestial.

–aa-duhl

(2) addle, paddle, saddle, straddle. (3) astraddle, skedaddle, unsaddle. (4) fiddle-faddle.

–aan-duhl

(2) candle, dandle, handle, sandal, scandal, vandal. (3) manhandle, mishandle, panhandle.

–ah-duhl

(2) coddle, model, noddle, swaddle, toddle, twaddle, waddle.
(3) remodel. (4) mollycoddle.

–aw-duhl

(2) caudal, dawdle.

–ay-duhl

(2) cradle, dreidel, ladle.

–ee-duhl

(2) beadle, needle, tweedle, wheedle.

–eh-duhl

(2) heddle, medal, meddle, pedal, peddle, treadle. (3) backpedal.
(4) intermeddle.

–ei-duhl

(2) bridal, bridle, idle, idol, idyll, sidle, tidal. (4) fratricidal, germicidal, herbicidal, homicidal, matricidal, parricidal, regicidal, suicidal. (5) infanticidal, insecticidal.

–i-duhl

(2) diddle, fiddle, griddle, piddle, riddle, twiddle.

–in-duhl

(2) brindle, dwindle, kindle, spindle, swindle. (3) enkindle, rekindle.

–oh-duhl

(2) modal, nodal, yodel.

–oo-duhl

(2) boodle, doodle, feudal, noodle, strudel. (3) caboodle, flapdoodle. (4) Yankee Doodle.

–oy-duhl

(3) colloidal, spheroidal, steroidal. (4) asteroidal, ellipsoidal, trapezoidal.

–uh-duhl

(2) cuddle, huddle, muddle, puddle, ruddle.

–uhn-duhl

(2) bundle, rundle, trundle.

–uhr-duhl

(2) curdle, girdle, hurdle.

–aa-fuhl

(2) baffle, raffle, snaffle.

–ah-fuhl

(2) offal, waffle.

–ahrt-fuhl

(2) artful, cartful.

–aw-fuhl

(2) awful, lawful. (3) unlawful.

–aym-fuhl

(2) blameful, shameful.

–ayn-fuhl

(2) baneful, gainful, painful. (3) disdainful.

–ayt-fuhl

(2) fateful, grateful, hateful, plateful.

–eed-fuhl

(2) heedful, needful.

–ehkt-fuhl

(3) neglectful, respectful. (4) disrespectful.

–ehnt-fuhl

(2) eventful, resentful. (3) uneventful.

–ehs-fuhl

(2) stressful. (3) distressful, successful. (4) unsuccessful.

–ei-fuhl

(2) Eiffel, eyeful, rifle, stifle, trifle.

–eit-fuhl

(2) frightful, rightful, spiteful. (3) delightful, insightful.

–i-fuhl

(2) piffle, riffle, sniffle, whiffle.

–il-fuhl

(2) skillful, willful. (3) unskillful.

–ir-fuhl

(2) cheerful, earful, fearful.

–ohl-fuhl

(2) bowlful, doleful, soulful.

–ohrn-fuhl

(2) mournful, scornful.

–oothh-fuhl

(2) ruthful, truthful, youthful.

–uh-fuhl

(2) duffle, muffle, ruffle, scuffle, shuffle, snuffle, truffle.

–aa-guhl

(2) daggle, draggle, gaggle, haggle, straggle, waggle. (3) bedraggle. (4) raggle-taggle.

–aang-guhl

(2) angle, bangle, dangle, jangle, mangle, spangle, strangle, tangle, wangle, wrangle. (3) bespangle, embrangle, entangle, quadrangle, rectangle, triangle, untangle, wide-angle. (4) disentangle.

–ah-guhl

(2) boggle, goggle, joggle, toggle. (3) boondoggle, hornswoggle.

–ee-guhl

(2) eagle, beagle, legal, regal. (3) illegal, vice-regal. (4) legal eagle, paralegal.

–i-guhl

(2) giggle, higgle, jiggle, niggle, sniggle, squiggle, wiggle, wriggle.

–ing-guhl

(2) cringle, dingle, ingle, jingle, mingle, shingle, single, tingle. (3) commingle, Kris Kringle, surcingle. (4) intermingle.

–oh-guhl

(2) bogle, Gogol, ogle.

–oo-guhl

(2) bugle, frugal, fugal, kugel.

–uh-guhl

(2) juggle, smuggle, snuggle, struggle.

–uhng-guhl

(2) bungle, jungle.

–uhr-guhl

(2) burgle, gurgle.

–aa-juhl

(2) agile, fragile.

–i-**juhl**

(2) sigil, strigil, vigil.

–aa-**kuhl**

(2) cackle, crackle, hackle, macle, shackle, spackle, tackle.
(3) ramshackle, unshackle. (4) tabernacle.

–aang-**kuhl**

(2) ankle, rankle.

–aak-**kuhl**

(2) paschal, rascal.

–ahr-**kuhl**

(2) darkle, sparkle. (3) monarchal. (4) matriarchal, patriarchal.

–eh-**kuhl**

(2) deckle, freckle, heckle, shekel, speckle. (4) Doctor Jekyll.

–i-**kuhl**

(2) chicle, fickle, mickle, nickel, pickle, prickle, sickle, stickle, tickle, trickle. (3) bicycle, icicle, tricycle, vehicle. (4) pumpernickel.

–ing-**kuhl**

(2) crinkle, inkle, sprinkle, tinkle, twinkle, winkle, wrinkle.
(3) besprinkle. (4) periwinkle.

–oh-**kuhl**

(2) focal, local, vocal, yokel. (3) bifocal, trifocal.

–uh-**kuhl**

(2) buckle, chuckle, knuckle, suckle, truckle. (3) Arbuckle, bare-knuckle, pinochle, swashbuckle, unbuckle, white-knuckle.
(4) honeysuckle.

–aa-**muhl**

(2) camel, mammal, Tamil, trammel. (3) enamel.

–iz-**muhl**

(2) dismal. (3) abysmal, baptismal. (4) cataclysmal, catechismal, paroxysmal.

–ohr-**muhl**

(2) formal, normal. (3) abnormal, informal, subnormal.
(4) paranormal.

–uhr-**muhl**

(2) dermal, thermal.

–aa-**nuhl**

(2) cannel, channel, flannel, panel.

–aap-**nuhl**

(2) grapnel, shrapnel.

–ahr-**nuhl**

(2) carnal, charnel, darnel.

–ee-**nuhl**

(2) penal, renal, venal. (3) adrenal.

–eh-**nuhl**

(2) fennel, kennel. (3) antennal.

–ei-**nuhl**

(2) final, spinal, trinal, vinyl. (4) anticlinal, officinal, semifinal.

–oh-**nuhl**

(2) clonal, tonal, zonal. (3) atonal, hormonal.

–uh-**nuhl**

(2) Chunnel, funnel, gunnel, gunwale, runnel, tunnel.

–uhm-**nuhl**

(3) autumnal, columnal.

–uhr-**nuhl**

(2) colonel, journal, kernel, sternal, urinal, vernal. (3) diurnal, eternal, external, fraternal, hibernal, infernal, internal, maternal, nocturnal, paternal, supernal.

–aa-**puhl**

(2) apple, chapel, dapple, grapple, scrapple. (3) pineapple.
(4) Adam's apple.

–aam-puhl

(2) ample, sample, trample. (3) ensample, example.

–ah-puhl

(2) stopple, topple. (3) estoppel.

–ay-puhl

(2) maple, papal, staple.

–ee-puhl

(2) people, steeple.

–ei-puhl

(3) disciple. (4) archetypal.

–i-puhl

(2) cripple, nipple, ripple, stipple, tipple, triple.

–im-puhl

(2) crimple, dimple, pimple, simple, wimple.

–oh-puhl

(2) opal, copal. (5) Constantinople.

–oo-puhl

(2) pupil, scruple. (3) quadruple, quintuple, sextuple.

–uh-puhl

(2) couple, supple.

–uhm-puhl

(2) crumple, rumple.

–aa-suhl

(2) castle, facile, hassle, passel, tassel, vassal. (3) forecastle, Newcastle.

–ah-suhl

(2) docile, dossal, fossil, jostle, throstle, wassail. (3) apostle, colossal.

–ahn-suhl

(2) consul, tonsil. (3) proconsul.

–ahr-**suhl**

(2) parcel, tarsal. (4) metatarsal.

–ehn-**suhl**

(2) mensal, pencil, pensile, stencil, tensile. (3) extensile, prehensile, utensil.

–eh-**suhl**

(2) nestle, pestle, trestle, vessel, wrestle.

–i-**suhl**

(2) bristle, fissile, gristle, missal, missile, scissile, thistle, whistle. (3) abyssal, dickcissel, dismissal, epistle.

–ohr-**suhl**

(2) dorsal, foresail, morsel.

–own-**suhl**

(2) council, counsel, groundsel.

–uh-**suhl**

(2) bustle, hustle, muscle, mussel, rustle, tussle.

–uhr-**suhl**

(2) bursal, tercel, tiercel, versal. (3) rehearsal, reversal, transversal. (4) universal.

–ahr-**shuhl**

(2) marshal, Marshall, martial, partial. (3) court martial, impartial.

–ay-**shuhl**

(2) facial, glacial, racial, spatial. (3) abbatial, palatial.

–ehn-**shuhl**

(3) agential, credential, essential, potential, prudential, sentential, sequential, tangential, torrential. (4) confidential, consequential, deferential, differential, evidential, existential, exponential, inferential, influential, influential, penitential, pestilential, preferential, presidential, providential, quintessential, referential, reverential, unessential. (5) circumferential, equipotential, experiential, inconsequential.

–i-shuhl

(3) comitial, initial, judicial, official. (4) artificial, beneficial, interstitial, prejudicial, sacrificial, superficial.

–ah-stuhl

(2) costal, hostel, hostile. (4) intercostal, Pentecostal.

–oh-stuhl

(2) coastal, postal.

–aa-tuhl

(2) battle, cattle, chattel, prattle, rattle, tattle. (3) embattle, Seattle.

–aak-tuhl

(2) dactyl, tactile. (3) contractile, protractile, retractile. (4) pterodactyl.

–aan-tuhl

(3) cantle, mantel, mantle. (4) dismantle.

–ah-tuhl

(2) bottle, dottle, glottal, mottle, pottle, throttle, wattle.
(3) bluebottle. (4) Aristotle.

–ay-tuhl

(2) fatal, natal. (3) postnatal. (4) antenatal, neonatal.

–ee-tuhl

(2) beetle, fetal.

–eh-tuhl

(2) fettle, Gretel, kettle, metal, mettle, nettle, petal, settle.
(3) unsettle.

–ehk-tuhl

(2) sectile. (3) erectile, insectile, projectile.

–ehn-tuhl

(2) cental, dental, gentle, lentil, mental, rental. (3) fragmental, parental, placental, segmental. (4) accidental, alimental, complemental, continental, departmental, detrimental, elemental, fundamental, governmental, incidental, instrumental, monumental, occidental, oriental, ornamental, regimental, rudimental, sacramental, supplemental, temperamental, transcendental. (5) coincidental, developmental, experimental, impedimental, transcontinental. (6) intercontinental.

–ehs-tuhl

(2) festal, vestal.

–ei- tuhl

(2) title, vital. (3) entitle, recital, requital, subtitle.

–i-tuhl

(2) brittle, kittle, little, skittle, spittle, tittle, victual, vittle, whittle. (3) acquittal, belittle, committal, lickspittle, remittal, transmittal.

–in-tuhl

(2) lintel, pintle, quintal.

–oh-tuhl

(2) dotal, total. (3) teetotal. (4) anecdotal, antidotal, sacerdotal.

–ohr-tuhl

(2) chortle, mortal, portal. (3) immortal.

–oo-tuhl

(2) brutal, futile, tootle. (3) inutile.

–uh-tuhl

(2) scuttle, shuttle, subtle. (3) rebuttal.

–uhn-tuhl

(2) frontal, gruntle. (3) disgruntle. (4) contrapuntal.

–uhr-tuhl

(2) fertile, hurtle, kirtle, myrtle, Myrtle, turtle. (3) infertile.

–eh-thhuhl

(2) Bethel, Ethel, ethyl, methyl.

–ahs-truhl

(2) costrel, nostril, rostral.

–ehs-truhl

(2) kestrel. (3) ancestral, fenestral, orchestral.

–aa-vuhl

(2) cavil, gavel, gravel, ravel, travel. (3) pea gravel, unravel.

–ah-vuhl

(2) grovel, hovel, novel.

–ahr-vuhl

(2) carvel, larval, marvel.

–ee-vuhl

(2) evil, weevil. (3) coeval, primeval, retrieval, upheaval.
(4) medieval.

–eh-vuhl

(2) bevel, devil, level, Neville, revel. (3) bedevil, dishevel.

–ei-vuhl

(2) rival. (3) arrival, revival, survival. (4) adjectival, conjunctival.
(5) imperatival.

–i-vuhl

(2) civil, drivel, shrivel, snivel, swivel.

–oo-vuhl

(3) approval, disproval, removal, reproval. (3) disapproval.

–aa-zuhl

(2) basil, Basil, dazzle, frazzle, razzle. (3) bedazzle. (4) razzle-dazzle.

–ah-zuhl

(2) nozzle, schnozzle.

–ay-zuhl

(2) basal, basil, hazel, nasal, phrasal. (3) appraisal, witch hazel.

–ee-zuhl

(2) diesel, easel, teasel, weasel.

–ei-**zuhl**

(3) reprisal. (4) paradisal.

–i-**zuhl**

(2) chisel, drizzle, fizzle, frizzle, grizzle, mizzle, sizzle, swizzle.

–oo-**zuhl**

(2) foozle, fusel, ouzel. (3) bamboozle, perusal, refusal.

–ow-**zuhl**

(2) housel, spousal, tousle. (3) arousal, carousal, espousal.

–uh-**zuhl**

(2) guzzle, muzzle, nuzzle, puzzle.

–**uhlch**

(1) cultch, gulch, mulch.

–**uhld**

–uhk-**uhld**

(2) cuckold.
ALSO: –**uh-kuhl** + -*ed* (i.e., *chuckled*, *swashbuckled*).

–i-**buhld**

(2) dibbled, dribbled, kibbled, nibbled, quibbled, ribald, scribbled.

–aa-**fuhld**

(2) baffled, raffled, scaffold, snaffled.

–ang-**guhld**

(2) angled, dangled, jangled, mangled, spangled, strangled, tangled, wangled, wrangled. (3) bespangled, embrangled, entangled, new-fangled, star-spangled, untangled. (4) disentangled.

–**uhlj**

(1) bulge. (2) divulge, effulge, indulge.

–**uhlk**

(1) bulk, hulk, skulk, sulk.

–**uhlp**

(1) gulp, pulp.

–uhls

(1) pulse. (2) convulse, impulse, repulse.

–uhlt

(1) cult. (2) adult, consult, exult, insult, occult, result, tumult.
(3) catapult, difficult. (4) antepenult.

–uhm

(1) bum, chum, come, crumb, drum, dumb, from, glum, hum, mum, numb, plum, plumb, rum, scum, slum, some, strum, sum, swum, thrum, thumb. (2) become, benumb, emblem, humdrum, pablum, spectrum, succumb, therefrom, wherefrom. (3) burdensome, Christendom, cranium, cumbersome, frolicsome, heathendom, kettledrum, laudanum, martyrdom, maximum, medium, mettlesome, minimum, modicum, odium, opium, optimum, overcome, pabulum, pendulum, platinum, podium, premium, quarrelsome, radium, speculum, sugar plum, tedium, troublesome, tympanum, venturesome, wearisome. (4) ad nauseam, adventuresome, aluminum, aquarium, chrysanthemum, compendium, continuum, curriculum, delirium, effluvium, emporium, encomium, exordium, geranium, gymnasium, harmonium, magnesium, millennium, opprobrium, palladium, petroleum, residuum, symposium. (5) auditorium, crematorium, equilibrium, pandemonium, sanitarium.

–ee-uhm

(3) lyceum, museum, per diem, Te Deum. (4) athenaeum, coliseum, mausoleum, (5) peritoneum.

–oh-uhm

(2) poem, proem. (4) jeroboam.

–ohr-uhm

(2) forum, quorum. (3) decorum. (4) indecorum, variorum.
(5) sanctum sanctorum.

–aa-duhm

(2) Adam, madam. (3) macadam.

–aan-duhm

(2) random, tandem. (3) memorandum.

–ehl-duhm

(2) beldam, seldom.

–ehn-duhm

(2) addendum, agendum, credendum, pudendum. (3) corrigendum, referendum.

–oh-kuhm

(2) hokum, locum, oakum.

–ah-luhm

(2) column, solemn.

–eh-luhm

(2) vellum. (3) flagellum. (4) antebellum, cerebellum.

–eh-nuhm

(2) denim, frenum, plenum, venom.

–aan-suhm

(2) handsome, hansom, ransom, transom.

–ah-suhm

(2) blossom, possum. (3) opossum.

–aan-tuhm

(2) bantam, phantom.

–ay-tuhm

(2) datum, stratum. (3) erratum, verbatim, substratum. (4) literatim, seriatim, ultimatum. (5) desideratum.

–oh-tuhm

(2) scrotum, totem. (3) factotum.

–ahs-truhm

(2) nostrum, rostrum.

–aa-zuhm

SEE: **–aazm**

–i-zuhm

SEE: **–izm**

–uhmp

(1) bump, chump, clump, dump, frump, grump, hump, jump, lump, mump, plump, pump, rump, slump, stump, thump, trump, ump. (2) mugwump.

–uhn

(1) bun, done, dun, fun, gun, Hun, none, nun, one, pun, run, shun, son, spun, stun, sun, ton, won. (2) begun, homespun, melon, outrun, rerun, someone, undone. (3) Albion, anyone, chamberlain, cinnamon, everyone, galleon, Galveston, garrison, halcyon, hit-and-run, Lucullan, orison, overdone, overrun, simpleton, singleton, skeleton, unison, venison. (4) accordion, comparison, oblivion, phenomenon.

–ee-uhn

(2) Ian, lien. (3) Aegean, Andean, Augean, Crimean, Judean, Korean, plebian, protean. (4) apogean, Caribbean, empyrean, European, Herculean, Jacobean, Manichean, Mycenaean, perigean, Sisyphean, Tenneseean. (5) antipodean, epicurean, Pythagorean, terpsichorean.

–ehr-uhn

(2) Aaron, baron, barren, Marin, Sharon.

–ehr-ee-uhn

(2) Arian, Aryan, carrion, clarion, Marian, Marion.

–ei-uhn

(2) Brian, ion, lion, scion, Zion. (3) anion, cation, Orion. (4) dandelion.

–ohr-uhn

(2) florin, foreign, warren.

–oo-uhn

(2) bruin, ruin.

–ah-buhn

(2) bobbin, Dobbin, robin, Robin.

–i-buhn

(2) gibbon, ribbon.

–uhr-buhn

(2) bourbon, turban, urban. (3) exurban, suburban. (4) interurban.

–ohr-chuhn

(2) fortune. (3) importune, misfortune.

–uhn-chuhn

(2) luncheon, puncheon, truncheon.

–uhr-chuhn

(2) birchen, urchin.

–uhs-chuhn

(2) fustian. (3) combustion.

–aa-duhn

(2) gladden, madden, sadden. (3) Aladdin.

–ah-duhn

(2) sodden, trodden. (3) downtrodden.

–ahr-duhn

(2) Arden, garden, harden, pardon. (3) beer garden, bombardon, caseharden.

–ay-duhn

(2) Aden, laden, maiden.

–eh-duhn

(2) deaden, leaden, redden. (4) Armageddon.

–ei-duhn

(2) guidon, widen. (3) Poseidon.

–i-duhn

(2) bidden, chidden, hidden, midden, ridden, stridden. (3) bedridden, forbidden, unbidden.

–ohl-duhn

(2) golden, olden. (3) beholden, embolden.

–ohr-duhn

(2) cordon, Gordon, Jordan, warden.

–ah-fuhn (–aw-fuhn)

(2) coffin, dauphin, often, soften.

–i-fuhn

(2) griffin, griffon, stiffen.

–uh-**fuhn**

(2) muffin, puffin, roughen, toughen. (4) ragamuffin.

–aa-**guhn**

(2) dragon, flagon, wagon. (3) bandwagon, pendragon, snapdragon.

–oh-**guhn**

(2) brogan, Hogan, shogun, slogan.

–ohr-**guhn**

(2) gorgon, Morgan, organ.

–ee-**juhn**

(2) legion, region. (3) collegian, Glaswegian, Norwegian.

–in-**juhn**

(2) Injun. (2) Carolingian.

–uh-**juhn**

(2) bludgeon, dudgeon, gudgeon. (3) curmudgeon.

–uhr-**juhn**

(2) burgeon, sturgeon, surgeon, virgin.

–aa-**kuhn**

(2) blacken, bracken, slacken.

–ahr-**kuhn**

(2) darken, hearken.

–ay-**kuhn**

(2) bacon, Macon, shaken, taken, waken. (3) awaken, forsaken, mistaken. (4) godforsaken.

–ee-**kuhn**

(2) beacon, deacon, weaken. (3) archdeacon, Mohican.

–eh-**kuhn**

(2) beckon, reckon.

–ei-**kuhn**

(2) lichen, liken.

–i-kuhn

(2) chicken, quicken, sicken, stricken, thicken, Wiccan.
(3) awestricken, fried chicken. (4) panic-stricken.

–oh-kuhn

(2) broken, oaken, spoken, token, woken. (3) bespoken, betoken, foretoken, heartbroken, housebroken, Hoboken, outspoken, plain-spoken, unbroken, unspoken.

–uhmp-kuhn

(2) bumpkin, pumpkin.

–uhr-kuhn

(2) firkin, gherkin, jerkin, merkin.

–uhs-kuhn

(2) buskin, Tuscan. (3) Etruscan, molluscan.

–aa-luhn

(2) Alan, Allen, Fallon, gallon, talon.

–eh-luhn

(2) Ellen, felon, Helen, melon. (3) Magellan, muskmelon.
(4) watermelon.

–ehm-luhn

(2) gremlin, Kremlin.

–oh-luhn

(2) colon, solon, Solon, stolen, swollen. (3) semicolon.

–aa-muhn

(2) famine, gamin, gammon, mammon, salmon. (3) backgammon, examine. (4) cross-examine, re-examine.

–ahch-muhn

(2) Scotchman, watchman.

–ay-muhn

(3) Cayman, Damon, drayman, layman, stamen.

–ee-muhn

(2) demon, freeman, leman, seaman, semen. (3) Philemon.

–ehnch-**muhn**

(2) Frenchman, henchman.

–ei-**muhn**

(2) hymen, limen, Lyman, pie-man, Simon.

–oh-**muhn**

(2) bowman, foeman, gnomon, omen, Roman, showman, yeoman.
(3) abdomen, cognomen.

–ohr-**muhn**

(2) doorman, foreman, Mormon, Norman. (3) longshoreman.

–oo-**muhn**

(2) crewman, human, lumen, Truman. (3) acumen, albumin, bitumen, illumine, inhuman. (4) catechumen, superhuman.

–uhr-**muhn**

(2) ermine, German, Herman, merman, sermon, Sherman.
(3) determine. (4) predetermine.

–eh-**nuhn**

(2) Lenin, pennon, tenon.

–ay-**puhn**

(2) capon. (3) misshapen.

–ee-**puhn**

(2) cheapen, deepen.

–ei-**ruhn**

(2) Byron, siren, Siren. (3) environ.

–aa-**suhn**

(2) fasten. (3) assassin, unfasten.

–aak-**suhn**

(2) flaxen, Jackson, klaxon, Saxon, waxen. (4) Anglo-Saxon.

–ahk-**suhn**

(2) coxswain, oxen.

–ahr-**suhn**

(2) arson, Carson, parson.

–ay-**suhn**

(2) basin, caisson, chasten, hasten, Jason, mason.

–i-**suhn**

(2) christen, glisten, listen.

–uhr-**suhn**

(2) person, worsen.

–aa-**shuhn**

(2) ashen, fashion, passion, ration. (3) compassion, dispassion, impassion.

–aak-**shuhn**

(2) action, faction, fraction, traction. (3) abstraction, attraction, compaction, contraction, detraction, distraction, exaction, extraction, inaction, infraction, protraction, reaction, redaction, refraction, retraction, subtraction, transaction. (4) benefaction, calefaction, counteraction, interaction, labefaction, malefaction, petrifaction, putrefaction, rarefaction, retroaction, satisfaction, stupefaction, tumefaction. (5) dissatisfaction.

–aan-**shuhn**

(2) mansion, scansion, stanchion. (3) expansion.

–aap-**shuhn**

(2) caption. (3) contraption.

–ahk-**shuhn**

(3) concoction, decoction.

–ahp-**shuhn**

(2) option. (3) adoption.

–aw-**shuhn**

(2) caution. (3) incaution, precaution.

–ay-shuhn

(2) Haitian, nation, ration, station. (3) ablation, aeration, carnation, castration, causation, cessation, citation, collation, creation, cremation, Dalmatian, damnation, deflation, dictation, dilation, donation, duration, elation, equation, filtration, fixation, flirtation, flotation, formation, foundation, frustration, gestation, gradation, gyration, inflation, lactation, laudation, lavation, legation, libation, location, migration, mutation, narration, negation, notation, oblation, oration, ovation, plantation, predation, privation, probation, prostration, pulsation, quotation, relation, rogation, rotation, sensation, serration, stagnation, taxation, temptation, translation, vacation, venation, vexation, vibration, vocation. (4) abdication, aberration, abjuration, abnegation, abrogation, acceptation, acclamation, accusation, actuation, adaptation, adjuration, admiration, adoration, adulation, adumbration, aerostation, affectation, affirmation, aggravation, aggregation, agitation, allegation, allocation, alteration, altercation, amputation, animation, annexation, annotation, appellation, application, approbation, arbitration, arrogation, aspiration, assignation, attestation, augmentation, aviation, avocation, bifurcation, calcinations, calculation, cancellation, captivation, castigation, celebration, circulation, cogitation, collocation, coloration, combination, commendation, commutation, compensation, compilation, complication, computation, concentration, condemnation, condensation, confirmation, confiscation, conflagration, conformation, confrontation, confutation, congregation, conjugation, conjuration, connotation, consecration, conservation, consolation, constellation, consternation, consultation, consummation, contemplation, conversation, convocation, copulation, coronation, corporation, correlation, corrugation, coruscation, culmination, debarkation, decimation, declamation, declaration, declination, decoration, dedication, defalcation, defamation, defloration, deformation, degradation, delectation, delegation, demonstration, denotation, denudation, depilation, deportation, depravation, deprecation, depredation, deprivation, deputation, derivation, derogation, desecration, desiccation, designation, desolation, desperation, destination, detestation, detonation, devastation, deviation, dislocation, dispensation, disputation, dissertation, dissipation, distillation, divination, domination, duplication, education, elevation, elongation, emanation, embarkation, emendation, emigration, emulation, enervation, equitation, eructation, estimation, evocation, exaltation, excavation, excitation, exclamation, execration,

exhalation, exhortation, expectation, expiation, expiration, explanation, explication, exploration, exportation, expurgation, extirpation, exultation, fabrication, fascination, federation, fenestration, fermentation, flagellation, fluctuation, fomentation, fornication, fulmination, fumigation, generation, germination, graduation, granulation, gravitation, habitation, hesitation, hibernation, ideation, illustration, imitation, implantation, implication, importation, imprecation, impregnation, incantation, incitation, inclination, incubation, inculcation, indentation, indication, indignation, infestation, infiltration, inflammation, information, inhalation, innovation, inspiration, installation, instigation, instillation, intimation, intonation, inundation, invitation, invocation, irrigation, irritation, isolation, jubilation, laceration, lamentation, legislation, levitation, liberation, limitation, litigation, lubrication, lucubration, maceration, machination, malformation, mastication, maturation, mediation, medication, meditation, menstruation, ministration, mitigation, moderation, modulation, molestation, mutilation, navigation, numeration, obfuscation, obligation, obscuration, observation, occupation, operation, ordination, orchestration, oscillation, palpitation, penetration, percolation, perforation, permeation, permutation, peroration, perpetration, perspiration, perturbation, population, postulation, predication, preparation, presentation, preservation, proclamation, procreation, profanation, prolongation, protestation, provocation, publication, punctuation, radiation, recitation, reclamation, recreation, reformation, refutation, registration, regulation, relaxation, remonstration, renovation, reparation, reputation, reservation, resignation, respiration, restoration, retardation, revelation, revocation, ruination, rumination, rustication, salutation, scintillation, segmentation, segregation, separation, sequestration, simulation, situation, speculation, spoliation, stimulation, sublimation, subornation, suffocation, supplication, suppuration, suspiration, syncopation, termination, titillation, toleration, transformation, transplantation, transportation, trepidation, tribulation, triplication, usurpation, vaccination, vacillation, valuation, variation, vegetation, veneration, ventilation, vindication, violation, visitation, vitiation. (5) abbreviation, abomination, acceleration, accentuation, accommodation, accreditation, accumulation, adjudication, administration, adulteration, affiliation, agglutination, alienation, alleviation, alliteration, amalgamation, amplification, annihilation, annunciation, anticipation, appreciation, appropriation, approximation, argumentation, articulation, asphyxiation, assassination, assimilation, association, attenuation, authorization, calcification, calumniation, canonization, capitulation, carbonization, catechization, clarification, coagulation, codification, cohabitation, columniation, commemoration, commensuration, commiseration, communication, concatenation, conciliation, confederation, configuration, conglomeration, congratulation, consideration, consolidation, contamination, continuation, cooperation, coordination, corroboration, crystallization, debilitation, degeneration, deification, deliberation, delineation, denomination, denunciation, depopulation, depreciation, despoliation, determination, dilapidation, disapprobation, discoloration, discrimination, disfiguration, disinclination, disintegration, dissemination, disseveration, dissimilation, dissociation, documentation, domestication, edification, effectuation, ejaculation, elaboration, elimination, elucidation, emaciation, emancipation, emasculation, enumeration, enunciation, equalization, equilibration, equivocation, eradication, evacuation, evaporation, evisceration, exacerbation, exaggeration, examination, exasperation, excoriation, exhilaration, exoneration, expatiation, expectoration, expostulation, expropriation, extenuation, extermination, facilitation, falsification, felicitation, fertilization, fortification, fossilization, galvanization, gesticulation, glorification, gratification, habilitation, habituation, hallucination, harmonization, humiliation, hypothecation, idealization, illumination, imagination, immoderation, inauguration, incarceration, incineration, incorporation, incrimination, inebriation, infatuation, initiation, inoculation, insemination, insinuation, interpolation, interpretation, interrogation, intoxication, investigation, irradiation, justification, legalization, manifestation, manipulation, matriculation, melioration, misinformation, modernization, modification, mollification, moralization, mortification, multiplication, mystification, nasalization, negotiation, notification, obliteration, origination, organization, ossification, pacification, participation, perambulation, peregrination, perpetuation, precipitation, predestination, predomination, premeditation, preoccupation, prevarication, procrastination, prognostication, pronunciation, propitiation, purification, qualification, ramification, ratification, realization, reciprocation, recommendation, recrimination, rectification, recuperation, refrigeration, regeneration, regurgitation, reiteration, rejuvenation, remuneration, renunciation, representation, repudiation, resuscitation, retaliation, reverberation, sanctification, scarification, signification, solemnization, sophistication, specialization, specification, subordination, substantiation, symbolization, variegation, versification, vituperation, vivification, vociferation. (6) amelioration, beatification, circumnavigation, contra-indication, cross-examination, deterioration, differentiation, discontinuation, disqualification, diversification, electrification, excommunication, exemplification, experimentation, extemporization, identification, inconsideration, indemnification, individuation, misrepresentation, naturalization, personification, predetermination, prestidigitation, ratiocination, recapitulation, reconciliation, supererogation, tintinnabulation, transubstantiation. (7) spiritualization.

–ee-shuhn

(2) Grecian. (3) accretion, completion, concretion, deletion, depletion, excretion, Phoenician, repletion, secretion, Tahitian.

–eh-shuhn

(2) cession, freshen, session. (3) accession, aggression, bull session, compression, concession, confession, depression, digression, discretion, expression, impression, ingression, obsession, oppression, possession, precession, procession, profession, progression, recession, secession, succession, suppression, transgression. (4) decompression, indiscretion, intercession, prepossession, dispossession, repossession, retrocession, retrogression, self-expression, self-possession.

–ehk-shuhn

(2) lection, section. (3) affection, bisection, collection, complexion, confection, connection, convection, correction, defection, deflection, dejection, detection, direction, dissection, ejection, election, erection, infection, inflection, injection, inspection, midsection, objection, perfection, projection, protection, reflection, rejection, selection, subjection, subsection, trajection, trisection. (4) circumspection, disaffection, genuflection, imperfection, indirection, insurrection, interjection, introspection, misdirection, predilection, preselection, recollection, re-election, resurrection, retrospection, venesection, vivisection.

–ehm-**shuhn**

(2) emption. (3) exemption, pre-emption, redemption.

–ehn-**shuhn**

(2) gentian, mention, pension, tension. (3) abstention, ascension, attention, contention, convention, declension, detention, dimension, dissention, distension, extension, intention, invention, pretension, prevention, recension, retention, suspension. (4) apprehension, circumvention, comprehension, condescension, contravention, inattention, intervention, reprehension. (5) incomprehension, misapprehension.

–i-**shuhn**

(2) fission, mission. (3) addition, admission, ambition, attrition, audition, cognition, coition, commission, condition, contrition, edition, emission, fruition, Galician, ignition, logician, magician, monition, munition, musician, nutrition, omission, optician, partition, patrician, perdition, permission, petition, physician, position, remission, rendition, sedition, submission, suspicion, tactician, tradition, transition, transmission, tuition, volition. (4) abolition, acquisition, admonition, ammunition, apparition, apposition, coalition, competition, composition, definition, demolition, deposition, disposition, disquisition, ebullition, electrician, erudition, exhibition, expedition, exposition, extradition, imposition, inanition, inhibition, inquisition, intermission, intuition, manumission, obstetrician, opposition, parturition, politician, premonition, preposition, prohibition, proposition, recognition, repetition, requisition, rhetorician, statistician, superstition, supposition, transposition. (5) academician, arithmetician, decomposition, dialectician, geometrician, indisposition, interposition, juxtaposition, mathematician, metaphysician, predisposition, presupposition.

–ik-**shuhn**

(2) diction, fiction, friction. (3) addiction, affliction, confliction, constriction, conviction, depiction, eviction, infliction, nonfiction, prediction, reliction, restriction, transfixion. (4) benediction, contradiction, dereliction, interdiction, jurisdiction, malediction, metafiction, science fiction, valediction.

–oh-shuhn

(2) Goshen, lotion, motion, notion, ocean, potion. (3) commotion, devotion, emotion, promotion, remotion. (4) locomotion.

–ohr-shuhn

(2) portion, torsion. (3) abortion, apportion, contortion, distortion, extortion, proportion. (4) disproportion.

–oo-shuhn

(2) Lucian. (3) ablution, Aleutian, Confucian, dilution, locution, pollution, solution. (4) absolution, attribution, comminution, constitution, contribution, convolution, destitution, devolution, diminution, dissolution, distribution, elocution, evolution, execution, institution, involution, Lilliputian, persecution, prosecution, prostitution, resolution, restitution, retribution, revolution, Rosicrucian, substitution. (5) circumlocution, electrocution, irresolution, reconstitution, redistribution.

–uh-shuhn

(2) Prussian, Russian. (3) concussion, discussion, percussion.
(4) repercussion.

–uhk-shuhn

(2) fluxion, ruction, suction. (3) abduction, adduction, conduction, construction, deduction, defluxion, destruction, effluxion, induction, instruction, production, reduction, seduction. (4) deconstruction, introduction, misconstruction, reconstruction, reproduction. (5) overproduction, superinduction.

–uhl-shuhn

(3) compulsion, convulsion, emulsion, expulsion, impulsion, propulsion, repulsion, revulsion.

–uhmp-shuhn

(2) gumption. (3) assumption, consumption, resumption, resumption.

–uhnk-shuhn

(2) function, junction, unction. (3) compunction, conjunction, disjunction, dysfunction, expunction, injunction.

–uhr-**shuhn**

(2) tertian. (3) assertion, Cistercian, coercion, desertion, exertion, insertion.

–aa-**tuhn**

(2) batten, fatten, flatten, Latin, Patton, platen, satin. (3) Manhattan.

–ah-**tuhn**

(2) cotton, gotten, Groton, rotten. (3) begotten, forgotten, ill-gotten. (4) misbegotten.

–ahr-**tuhn**

(2) Barton, carton, hearten, marten, martin, Martin, smarten, Spartan, tartan. (3) dishearten. (4) kindergarten.

–ay-**tuhn**

(2) Satan, straighten, straiten.

–ee-**tuhn**

(2) beaten, Cretan, cretin, eaten, Eton, sweeten, wheaten.
(3) browbeaten, moth-eaten, unbeaten. (4) overeaten, weather-beaten.

–ehn-**tuhn**

(2) dentin, Lenten, Quentin, Trenton. (3) San Quentin.

–ehs-**tuhn**

(2) destine. (3) clandestine, intestine, predestine.

–ei-**tuhn**

(2) brighten, Brighton, frighten, heighten, lighten, tighten, Titan, triton, whiten. (3) enlighten.

–i-**tuhn**

(2) bitten, Britain, Briton, kitten, mitten, smitten, written.

–is-**tuhn**

(2) Kristin, piston, Tristan. (3) phlogiston, sacristan. (4) amethystine.

–oh-**tuhn**

(2) croton, oaten. (3) verboten.

–ohr-**tuhn**

(2) Horton, Morton, Norton, quartan, shorten.

–own-**tuhn**

(2) fountain, mountain.

–uh-**tuhn**

(2) button, glutton, mutton.

–uhr-**tuhn**

(2) Burton, certain, curtain, Merton. (3) uncertain.

–ehngh-**thuhn**

(2) lengthen, strengthen.

–ay-**truhn**

(2) matron, natron, patron.

–ay-**vuhn**

(2) craven, graven, haven, maven, raven, shaven. (3) New Haven.
(4) riboflavin.

–ee-**vuhn**

(2) even, Steven. (3) uneven.

–eh-**vuhn**

(2) Devon, heaven, leaven, seven. (3) eleven.

–i-**vuhn**

(2) driven, given, riven, shriven. (3) forgiven.

–oh-**vuhn**

(2) cloven, coven, woven. (3) Beethoven, hand-woven.
(4) interwoven.

–uh-**vuhn**

(2) coven, oven, sloven.

–aan-**yuhn**

(2) banyan, canyon. (3) companion.

–eel-**yuhn**

(2) Pelion. (3) aphelion, chameleon. (4) perihelion.

–il-yuhn

(2) billion, jillion, million, pillion, trillion, zillion. (3) Castilian, civilian, cotillion, gazillion, pavilion, postilion, quadrillion, Quintilian, quintillion, reptilian, vermilion. (4) crocodilian, Maximilian.

–in-yuhn

(2) minion, pinion, piñon. (3) dominion, opinion, Virginian.

–uhl-yuhn

(2) cullion, mullion, scullion.

–uhn-yuhn

(2) bunion, Bunyan, onion, Runyon, trunnion.

–ay-zuhn

(2) blazon, brazen, raisin. (3) emblazon, diapason.

–ee-zuhn

(2) reason, season, treason. (3) unreason.

–ei-zuhn

(2) bison, dizen. (3) bedizen, horizon.

–i-zuhn

(2) mizzen, prison, wizen. (3) arisen, imprison.

–oh-zuhn

(2) chosen, frozen, hosen.

–uh-zuhn

(2) cousin, cozen, dozen.

–ay-zhuhn

(2) Asian, suasion. (3) abrasion, Caucasian, dissuasion, equation, Eurasian, evasion, invasion, occasion, persuasion, pervasion. (4) Rabelaisian.

–ee-zhuhn

(2) Frisian, lesion. (3) adhesion, artesian, Cartesian, cohesion, Elysian, Parisian, Silesian. (4) Indonesian, Micronesian, Polynesian.

–i-**zhuhn**

(2) vision. (3) collision, concision, decision, derision, division, elision, Elysian, envision, excision, incision, misprision, precision, prevision, provision, recision, rescission, revision. (4) circumcision, subdivision, subincision, supervision, television, x-ray vision.

–oh-**zhuhn**

(2) Ambrosian, corrosion, erosion, explosion, implosion.

–oo-**zhuhn**

(2) fusion. (3) allusion, collusion, conclusion, confusion, contusion, delusion, diffusion, effusion, elusion, exclusion, extrusion, illusion, inclusion, infusion, intrusion, Malthusian, obtrusion, occlusion, profusion, protrusion, reclusion, seclusion, suffusion, transfusion. (4) disillusion, interfusion.

–uhr-**zhuhn**

(2) Persian, version. (3) aspersion, aversion, coercion, conversion, discursion, dispersion, diversion, excursion, immersion, incursion, inversion, perversion, reversion, submersion, subversion. (4) extro-version, introversion. (5) animadversion.

–uhnch

(1) brunch, bunch, crunch, hunch, lunch, munch, punch, scrunch.

–uhnd

(1) bund, fund, gunned, shunned, stunned. (2) fecund, jocund, obtund, refund, rotund. (3) cummerbund, moribund, orotund, rubicund.

–ehr-**uhnd**

(2) errand, gerund.

–eh-**kuhnd**

(2) beckoned, fecund, reckoned, second. (3) split-second.

–ei-**luhnd**

(2) island, highland, Thailand.

–in-**luhnd**

(2) inland, Finland, Greenland, Iceland.

–ei-**puhnd**

(2) ripened, stipend.

–ee-**zuhnd**

(2) reasoned, seasoned, weasand. (3) unseasoned.

–**uhng**

(1) Bung, clung, dung, flung, Hmong, hung, lung, rung, slung, sprung, strung, stung, sung, swung, tongue, wrung, young. (2) among, high-strung, Shantung, unstrung, unsung. (3) iron lung, overhung.

–**uhnkt**

(2) adjunct, defunct, disjunct.
ALSO: –**uhnk** + -*ed* (i.e., *flunked*, *spelunked*).

–**uhnj**

(1) lunge, plunge, sponge. (2) expunge. (3) muskellunge.

–**uhnk**

(1) bunk, chunk, drunk, dunk, flunk, funk, hunk, junk, monk, plunk, punk, shrunk, skunk, slunk, spunk, sunk, trunk. (2) kerplunk, Podunk, punch-drunk, spelunk.

–**uhns**

(1) dunce, once.

–ay-**uhns**

(2) abeyance, conveyance, purveyance.

–ei-**uhns**

(2) clients, giants, science. (3) affiance, alliance, appliance, compliance, defiance, reliance. (4) misalliance.

–ir-**uhns**

(2) clearance. (3) adherence, appearance, coherence, inherence.
(4) disappearance, incoherence, interference, perseverance.

–oy-**uhns**

(2) buoyance. (3) annoyance, clairvoyance, flamboyance.

–uur-**uhns**

(2) durance. (3) assurance, endurance, insurance. (4) reassurance.

–ee-duhns

(2) credence. (3) impedance, precedence. (4) antecedence.

–ehn-duhns

(2) tendance. (3) ascendance, attendance, dependence, resplendence, transcendence. (4) condescendence, independence.

–uhl-juhns

(3) effulgence, indulgence, refulgence. (4) self-indulgence.

–uhr-juhns

(2) convergence, divergence, emergence, resurgence, submergence.

–ay-suhns

(2) nascence. (3) complacence, complaisance, obeisance, renascence.

–eh-suhns

(2) essence. (3) candescence, excrescence, fluorescence, pubescence, putrescence, quiescence, quintessence, senescence, tumescence. (4) acquiescence, adolescence, coalescence, convalescence, deli-quescence, effervescence, efflorescence, evanescence, incandes-cence, iridescence, obsolescence, opalescence, phosphorescence, recrudescence. (5) preadolescence.

–ee-shuhns (–eh-shuhns)

(2) nescience, prescience.

–ehn-tuhns

(2) sentence, repentance.

–i-tuhns

(2) pittance, quittance. (3) acquittance, admittance, remittance, transmittance. (4) intermittence.

–is-tuhns

(2) distance. (3) assistance, consistence, existence, insistence, persistence, resistance, subsistence. (4) coexistence, equidistance, nonexistence, nonresistance.

–ei-vuhns

(3) connivance, contrivance, survivance.

–eh-**zuhns**

(2) pleasance, presence. (4) omnipresence.
ALSO: **–ehz-uhnt** + *-s* (i.e., *pheasants*, *presents*).

–**uhnt**

(1) blunt, brunt, bunt, front, grunt, hunt, punt, runt, shunt, stunt.
(2) affront, beachfront, confront, forefront, manhunt, storefront.

–ay-dee-**uhnt**

(2) gradient, radiant.

–ehr-**uhnt**

(2) arrant, errant, parent. (3) aberrant, apparent, knight-errant, transparent.

–ei-**uhnt**

(2) client, giant, pliant. (3) affiant, compliant, defiant, reliant.

–ohr-**uhnt**

(2) torrent, warrant. (3) abhorrent.

–oo-**uhnt**

(2) fluent, truant. (3) pursuant.

–oy-**uhnt**

(2) buoyant. (3) clairvoyant, flamboyant.

–uhm-**buhnt**

(3) decumbent, incumbent, procumbent, recumbent.

–ahn-**duhnt**

(2) fondant. (3) despondent, respondent. (4) co-respondent, correspondent.

–ee-**duhnt**

(2) credent, needn't. (3) decedent, precedent, succedent.
(4) antecedent.

–ehn-**duhnt**

(2) pendant, pendent, splendent. (3) appendant, ascendant, attendant, defendant, dependant, dependent, descendant, descendent, impendent, intendant, resplendent, transcendent. (4) independent. (5) interdependent, superintendent.

–ei-duhnt

(2) strident, trident.

–oo-duhnt

(2) prudent, student. (3) imprudent. (4) jurisprudent.

–uhn-duhnt

(3) abundant, redundant.

–aa-gruhnt

(2) flagrant, fragrant, vagrant.

–ahr-juhnt

(2) argent, sergeant.

–in-juhnt

(2) stringent. (3) astringent, constringent, contingent.

–uhl-juhnt

(2) fulgent. (3) effulgent, indulgent, refulgent. (4) self-indulgent.

–uhr-juhnt

(2) urgent. (3) abstergent, assurgent, convergent, detergent, divergent, emergent, insurgent, resurgent.

–ee-kuhnt

(2) piquant, secant. (3) cosecant.

–ay-luhnt

(2) assailant, covalent, inhalant, surveillant. (3) multivalent.

–aach-muhnt

(2) hatchment. (3) attachment.

–awl-muhnt

(3) enthrallment, installment. (4) disenthrallment.

–ay-muhnt

(2) claimant, payment, raiment. (3) defrayment, repayment.

–ayj-muhnt

(3) assuagement, engagement, enragement.

–ayl-**muhnt**

(2) ailment, bailment. (3) assailment, curtailment, derailment, entailment, impalement, regalement.

–ays-**muhnt**

(2) basement, casement, placement. (3) abasement, debasement, defacement, displacement, effacement, embracement, enlacement, misplacement, subbasement. (4) interlacement.

–ayv-**muhnt**

(2) pavement. (3) enslavement.

–eech-**muhnt**

(2) preachment. (3) impeachment.

–eel-**muhnt**

(3) concealment, congealment.

–ehnt-**muhnt**

(2) contentment, presentment, resentment. (3) discontentment.

–ein-**muhnt**

(3) alignment, assignment, confinement, consignment, entwinement, refinement.

–eit-**muhnt**

(3) excitement, incitement, indictment.

–ig-**muhnt**

(2) figment, pigment.

–oh-**muhnt**

(2) foment, moment. (3) bestowment.

–ohr-**muhnt**

(2) dormant. (3) conformant, informant.

–ohrt-**muhnt**

(3) assortment, comportment, deportment, disportment.

–oov-**muhnt**

(2) movement. (3) improvement.

–oy-**muhnt**

(3) deployment, employment, enjoyment. (4) unemployment.

–oynt-**muhnt**

(2) ointment. (3) anointment, appointment. (4) disappointment.

–uhr-**muhnt**

(2) ferment. (3) allurement, averment, conferment, deferment, determent, immurement, interment, preferment, procurement. (4) disinterment.

–eh-**nuhnt**

(2) pennant, tenant. (3) lieutenant.

–ehg-**nuhnt**

(2) pregnant, regnant.

–ig-**nuhnt**

(3) benignant, indignant, malignant.

–oh-**nuhnt**

(2) sonant. (3) component, deponent, exponent, opponent, proponent.

–ei-**ruhnt**

(2) spirant, tyrant. (3) aspirant.

–ay-**suhnt**

(2) nascent. (3) adjacent, complacent, complaisant, renascent, subjacent. (4) circumjacent.

–ee-**suhnt**

(2) decent, puissant, recent. (3) indecent, obeisant.

–eh-**suhnt**

(2) crescent, jessant. (3) candescent, depressant, excrescent, fluorescent, ignescent, incessant, liquescent, putrescent, quiescent, senescent. (4) adolescent, convalescent, deliquescent, detumescent, effervescent, efflorescent, evanescent, incandescent, luminescent, obsolescent, opalescent, phosphorescent, recrudescent. (5) antidepressant.

–oo-**suhnt**

(2) lucent. (3) abducent, translucent.

–i-**shuhnt**

(3) deficient, efficient, omniscient, proficient, sufficient.
(4) coefficient, inefficient, insufficient.

–ay-**tuhnt**

(2) blatant, latent.

–ehk-**tuhnt**

(2) expectant. (3) disinfectant.

–ehks-**tuhnt**

(2) extant, sextant.

–uhr-**vuhnt**

(2) fervent, servant. (3) observant. (4) unobservant.

–il-**yuhnt**

(2) brilliant. (3) resilient.

–eh-**zuhnt**

(2) peasant, pheasant, pleasant, present. (3) unpleasant.
(4) omnipresent.

–**uhp**

(1) cup, pup, sup, up. (2) backup, bang-up, blowup, built-up, catch-up, checkup, fill-up, foul-up, grownup, hiccup, makeup, mock-up, setup, sit-up, slipup, teacup, thumbs-up, tossup, touchup, trumped-up, tune-up, washed-up, windup. (3) buttercup, cover-up, higher-up, pick-me-up, runner-up. (4) sunny-side up.

–uhr-**uhp**

(2) chirrup, stirrup, syrup.

–aa-**luhp**

(2) gallop, jalap, scallop, shallop. (3) escallop.

–ah-**luhp**

(2) dollop, lollop, scallop, trollop, wallop.

−eh-**luhp**

(3) develop, envelop.

−oo-**luhp**

(2) julep, tulip.

−**uhpt**

(2) abrupt, corrupt, disrupt, erupt. (3) interrupt.
ALSO: −**uhp** + -*ed* (i.e., *cupped*, *hiccupped*).

−**uhr**

(1) blur, bur, burr, coeur, cur, fir, fur, her, myrrh, per, purr, shirr, sir, slur, spur, stir, sure, were, whir. (2) astir, archer, aver, Ben Hur, Big Sur, chasseur, chauffeur, coiffeur, color, concur, confer, defer, demur, deter, donor, furor, hauteur, incur, infer, inter, jongleur, junior, juror, larkspur, lessor, liqueur, manor, mature, mister, occur, prefer, recur, refer, seigneur, senior, transfer, unsure, vendor, worker. (3) amateur, ancestor, arbiter, auditor, barrister, bachelor, calendar, chancellor, chronicler, chorister, colander, comforter, connoisseur, conqueror, creditor, counselor, cylinder, de rigueur, dowager, editor, emperor, gossamer, governor, guarantor, harbinger, immature, janitor, Jennifer, Jupiter, lavender, Lucifer, mariner, massacre, messenger, minister, monitor, monsignor, officer, orator, passenger, prisoner, raconteur, register, scimitar, senator, sepulcher, theatre, traveler, visitor, voyager, voyageur, warrior. (4) ambassador, administer, astrologer, astronomer, barometer, competitor, depositor, entrepreneur, Excalibur, executor, idolater, inheritor, inquisitor, progenitor, proprietor, restaurateur, solicitor, thermometer.

−aang-**uhr**

(2) banger, clangor, ganger, hangar, hanger. (3) haranguer, straphanger.

−ay-**uhr**

(2) layer, mayor, prayer. (3) purveyor, soothsayer, surveyor.
ALSO: −**ay** + -*er* (i.e., *player*, *naysayer*).

−ehr-ee-**uhr**

(2) barrier, burier, carrier, charier, harrier, merrier, terrier.

–ei-**uhr**

(2) briar, brier, buyer, choir, crier, dire, drier, dryer, dyer, fire, flier, flyer, friar, fryer, gyre, higher, hire, ire, liar, lyre, mire, prior, pyre, quire, shire, shyer, sire, slyer, spire, spryer, squire, tire, Tyre, wire. (3) acquire, admire, afire, aspire, attire, bemire, bonfire, conspire, desire, empire, enquire, entire, esquire, expire, grandsire, hot-wire, inquire, inspire, perspire, quagmire, require, respire, retire, sapphire, satire, spitfire, supplier, transpire, vampire, wildfire. (4) amplifier, beautifier, classifier, crucifier, glorifier, justifier, magnifier, multiplier, pacifier, purifier, qualifier, verifier. (5) disqualifier, humidifier, identifier.
ALSO: –ei + -er (i.e., *humidifier*).

–in-ee-**uhr**

(2) finnier, linear, skinnier. (3) nonlinear.

–ing-**uhr**

(2) bringer, flinger, ringer, singer, slinger, stinger, stringer, wringer. (3) folksinger, gunslinger, humdinger, left-winger, mudslinger, right-winger. (4) Meistersinger, minnesinger.

–iz-ee-**uhr**

(2) busier, dizzier, frizzier, vizier.

–oh-**uhr**

(2) blower, crower, grower, knower, lower, mower, ower, rower, sewer, slower, sower, thrower.

–ohr-**uhr**

(2) borer, corer, horror, scorer, snorer. (3) abhorrer, adorer, explorer, ignorer, restorer.

–oo-**uhr**

(2) brewer, ewer, fewer, hewer, skewer, sewer, viewer.

–ow-**uhr**

(2) bower, cower, dour, dower, flour, flower, glower, hour, lour, our, power, scour, shower, sour, tower. (3) cornflower, deflower, devour, embower, empower, horsepower, manpower, mayflower, safflower, sunflower, wallflower, watchtower, wildflower, willpower. (4) cauliflower, Eisenhower, overpower, passionflower, Schopenhauer, superpower, sweet-and-sour, thundershower, waterpower.

–oy-uhr

(2) foyer, lawyer. (3) annoyer, destroyer, employer, enjoyer, Tom Sawyer.

–uur-uhr

(2) curer, fuehrer, furor, juror, purer. (3) abjurer, insurer, procurer, securer.

–aa-buhr

(2) blabber, clabber, dabber, drabber, grabber, jabber, nabber, stabber.

–aam-buhr

(2) amber, camber, clamber, tambour.

–ah-buhr

(2) clobber, cobber, jobber, lobber, robber, slobber, sober, swabber.

–ahr-buhr

(2) arbor, barber, harbor.

–ay-buhr

(2) caber, labor, neighbor, saber, tabor. (3) belabor.

–ehm-buhr

(2) ember, member. (3) December, dismember, November, remember, September. (4) disremember.

–ei-buhr

(2) briber, fiber, giber, Tiber. (3) imbiber, inscriber, prescriber, subscriber, transcriber.

–i-buhr

(2) bibber, cribber, dibber, fibber, gibber, glibber, jibber. (3) ad-libber.

–im-buhr

(2) limber, timber, timbre.

–oh-buhr

(2) prober, sober. (3) disrober, October.

–uh-buhr

(2) blubber, clubber, drubber, dubber, grubber, lubber, rubber, scrubber, snubber. (3) landlubber. (4) money-grubber. (5) India rubber.

–uhm-buhr

(2) cumber, lumbar, lumber, number, slumber, umber.
(3) cucumber, encumber, outnumber, renumber. (4) disencumber.

–aa-chuhr

(2) catcher, matcher, scratcher, snatcher, stature, thatcher.
(3) backscratcher, dispatcher, detacher, dogcatcher, flycatcher.

–aak-chuhr

(2) fracture. (4) manufacture.

–ah-chuhr

(2) botcher, watcher.

–ahr-chuhr

(2) archer, marcher. (3) departure.

–ay-chuhr

(2) nature. (4) legislature, nomenclature.

–ee-chuhr

(2) bleacher, creature, feature, preacher, teacher. (3) beseecher, impeacher.

–eh-chuhr

(2) etcher, fetcher, fletcher, lecher, retcher, sketcher, stretcher.

–ehk-chuhr

(2) lecture. (3) conjecture, prefecture. (4) architecture.

–ehn-chuhr

(2) bencher, blencher, censure, clencher, denture, quencher, trencher, venture, wencher. (3) adventure, debenture, indenture, jaw-clencher. (4) misadventure, peradventure.

–es-chuhr

(2) gesture. (3) divesture.

–i-chuhr

(2) ditcher, hitcher, pitcher, richer, stitcher, switcher.

–in-chuhr

(2) clincher, flincher, lyncher, pincher, pinscher. (3) penny-pincher.

–ik-**chuhr**

(2) picture, stricture, depicture.

–iks-**chuhr**

(2) fixture, mixture. (3) admixture, commixture, immixture.
(4) intermixture.

–ink-**chuhr**

(2) cincture, tincture. (3) encincture.

–ohr-**chuhr**

(2) scorcher, torture.

–oo-**chuhr**

(2) future, moocher, suture.

–ow-**chuhr**

(2) croucher, sloucher, voucher.

–uhl-**chuhr**

(2) culture, vulture. (3) agriculture, aviculture, floriculture,
horticulture, pisciculture, viniculture.

–uhnk-**chuhr**

(2) juncture, puncture. (3) conjuncture.

–aa-**duhr**

(2) adder, bladder, gladder, ladder, madder, sadder. (3) stepladder.

–aan-**duhr**

(2) candor, dander, gander, grander, pander, sander, slander.
(3) backhander, bystander, commander, dittander, meander,
philander, pomander. (4) Alexander, coriander, gerrymander,
oleander, salamander.

–ah-**duhr**

(2) dodder, fodder, nodder, odder, plodder, prodder, solder.

–ahn-**duhr**

(2) blonder, bonder, condor, fonder, ponder, squander, wander,
yonder. (3) absconder, responder.

–ahr-**duhr**

(2) ardor, carder, harder, larder.

–awn-**duhr**

(2) launder, maunder.

–ay-**duhr**

(2) grader, raider, seder, trader. (3) crusader, Darth Vader, evader, invader persuader.

–ayn-**duhr**

(2) attainder, remainder.

–ehl-**duhr**

(2) elder, welder.

–ehn-**duhr**

(2) bender, blender, fender, gender, lender, render, sender, slender, spender, splendor, tender, vendor. (3) amender, ascender, bartender, contender, defender, emender, engender, extender, offender, pretender, surrender, suspender, weekender. (4) moneylender.

–ei-**duhr**

(2) cider, eider, glider, guider, hider, rider, spider, wider. (3) backslider, confider, divider, insider, outrider, outsider, provider.

–il-**duhr**

(2) builder, gilder, guilder. (3) bewilder.

–in-**duhr**

(2) cinder, tinder. (3) rescinder.

–oh-**duhr**

(2) loader, Oder, odor. (3) breechloader, corroder, exploder, foreboder, freeloader, malodor. (4) muzzleloader.

–ohl-**duhr**

(2) bolder, boulder, colder, folder, holder, molder, older, shoulder, smolder. (3) beholder, householder, upholder.

–ohr-**duhr**

(2) boarder, border, hoarder, order, warder. (3) disorder, recorder, rewarder.

–ow-**duhr**

(2) chowder, crowder, louder, powder, prouder.

–own-**duhr**

(2) bounder, flounder, founder, pounder, rounder, sounder.
(3) confounder, expounder, propounder.

–oy-**duhr**

(2) avoider, embroider.

–uh-**duhr**

(2) flooder, rudder, shudder, udder.

–uhn-**duhr**

(2) blunder, sunder, thunder, under, wonder. (3) asunder, thereunder.

–uhr-**duhr**

(2) girder, herder, murder. (3) sheepherder.

–aa-**fuhr**

(2) chaffer, gaffer, laugher.

–ah-**fuhr** (–aw-**fuhr**)

(2) coffer, cougher, doffer, goffer, offer, proffer, scoffer.

–ay-**fuhr**

(2) safer, wafer. (3) cockchafer.

–eh-**fuhr**

(2) deafer, feoffer, heifer, zephyr.

–ei-**fuhr**

(2) cipher, fifer, lifer, rifer. (3) decipher.

–uh-**fuhr**

(2) bluffer, buffer, duffer, gruffer, huffer, puffer, rougher, snuffer, stuffer, suffer, tougher.

–aa-**guhr**

(2) bagger, bragger, dagger, gagger, jagger, nagger, wager.
(4) agar-agar, carpetbagger.

–aang-**guhr**

(2) anger, languor.

–ahng-guhr (–awng-guhr)

(2) conger, longer, stronger.

–ee-guhr

(2) eager, leaguer, meager. (3) beleaguer, intriguer. (4) overeager.

–eh-guhr

(2) beggar, egger. (3) bootlegger.

–i-guhr

(2) bigger, chigger, digger, jigger, rigger, rigor, swigger, trigger, vigor. (3) gold digger, gravedigger, outrigger.

–ing-guhr

(2) finger, linger. (3) malinger.

–uh-guhr

(2) bugger, hugger, smugger, snugger.

–uhl-guhr

(2) Bulgar, bulgur, vulgar.

–uhng-guhr

(2) hunger, monger, younger. (3) gossipmonger, newsmonger.

–aa-juhr

(2) badger, cadger.

–ah-juhr

(2) codger, dodger, Dodger, lodger, Roger.

–ahr-juhr

(2) charger, larger. (3) enlarger.

–ay-juhr

(2) major, pager, sager, stager. (3) assuager.

–ayn-juhr

(2) changer, danger, granger, manger, ranger, stranger. (3) arranger, bushranger, endanger, estranger, exchanger. (4) disarranger, interchanger, moneychanger.

–eh-juhr

(2) dredger, edger, hedger, ledger.

–in-juhr

(2) cringer, ginger, injure. (3) harbinger, infringer.

–ohr-juhr

(2) forger, gorger, ordure. (3) disgorger.

–uhn-juhr

(2) lunger, plunger, sponger. (3) expunger.

–uhr-juhr

(2) merger, perjure, verdure, verger.

–aa-kuhr

(2) backer, clacker, cracker, hacker, lacquer, packer, slacker.
(3) hijacker, nutcracker. (4) Green Bay Packer.

–aang-kuhr

(2) anchor, banker, blanker, canker, chancre, danker, hanker, rancor,
ranker, spanker, tanker. (3) co-anchor.

–ah-kuhr

(2) blocker, clocker, cocker, docker, knocker, locker, mocker,
rocker, shocker, soccer, stocker. (4) beta blocker, knickerbocker.

–ay-kuhr

(2) acre, baker, breaker, faker, fakir, maker, Quaker, shaker, Shaker,
taker. (3) bookmaker, dressmaker, heartbreaker, lawbreaker, match-
maker, pacemaker, peacemaker, snowmaker, tiebreaker, watch-
maker, windbreaker. (4) boilermaker, circuit breaker, undertaker.

–eh-kuhr

(2) checker, pecker, trekker, wrecker. (3) exchequer, woodpecker.
(4) double-decker, rubbernecker.

–i-kuhr

(2) bicker, dicker, flicker, kicker, knicker, licker, liquor, picker,
quicker, sicker, slicker, snicker, thicker, ticker, vicar, wicker.
(3) bootlicker, nitpicker.

–ing-kuhr

(2) blinker, clinker, drinker, inker, shrinker, sinker, stinker, thinker,
tinker, winker.

–is-**kuhr**

(2) brisker, frisker, risker, whisker.

–oh-**kuhr**

(2) broker, choker, croaker, joker, ocher, poker, soaker, smoker, stoker, stroker. (3) convoker, evoker, invoker, provoker, revoker, stockbroker. (4) mediocre.

–oo-**kuhr**

(2) euchre, lucre, puker. (3) rebuker.

–uh-**kuhr**

(2) bucker, chucker, ducker, mucker, pucker, succor, sucker, trucker, tucker. (3) sapsucker, seersucker.

–uhng-**kuhr**

(2) bunker, drunker, dunker, junker, punker.

–uhr-**kuhr**

(2) jerker, lurker, shirker, worker.

–aa-**luhr**

(2) pallor, valor.

–aamp-**luhr**

(2) ampler, sampler.

–aand-**luhr**

(2) chandler, dandler, handler. (3) panhandler.

–aant-**luhr**

(2) antler. (3) dismantler.

–aat-**luhr**

(2) battler, rattler, tattler.

–ah-**luhr**

(2) choler, collar, dollar, scholar, squalor.

–ahb-**luhr**

(2) cobbler, gobbler, squabbler, wobbler.

–ahs-**luhr**

(2) hostler, jostler, ostler, wassailer.

–aw-luhr

(2) baller, caller, taller, smaller.

–ay-luhr

(2) gaoler, jailer, paler, sailer, sailor, staler, tailor, trailer, whaler.
(3) blackmailer, retailer, wholesaler.

–eh-luhr

(2) cellar, dweller, feller, seller, smeller, speller, stellar, teller.
(3) bestseller, expeller, foreteller, impeller, propeller, rathskeller,
root cellar. (4) fortune teller, interstellar, Rockefeller, storyteller.

–ehd-luhr

(2) meddler, medlar, peddler, pedlar.

–ehmp-luhr

(2) templar. (3) exemplar.

–i-luhr

(2) chiller, driller, filler, griller, killer, miller, pillar, spiller, swiller,
thriller, tiller. (3) distiller, Mankiller. (4) caterpillar, lady-killer.

–oh-luhr

(2) bowler, coaler, droller, molar, polar, poller, roller, solar, stroller,
troller. (3) cajoler, comptroller, consoler, controller, enroller, extol-
ler, patroller, bankroller, steamroller.

–uh-luhr

(2) color, cruller, culler, duller, sculler. (3) discolor, medullar,
off-color, tricolor. (4) Technicolor, multicolor, watercolor.

–uhd-luhr

(2) cuddler, huddler, muddler.

–uhk-luhr

(2) buckler, chuckler, knuckler. (3) swashbuckler.

–uhr-luhr

(2) curler, hurler, twirler.

–uhs-luhr

(2) hustler, rustler.

–uht-**luhr**

(2) butler, cutler, subtler.

–uhz-**luhr**

(2) guzzler, muzzler, puzzler.

–aa-**muhr**

(2) clamor, crammer, glamour, grammar, hammer, rammer, slammer, stammer, yammer. (3) enamor, jackhammer, programmer, sledgehammer, windjammer. (4) katzenjammer, ninnyhammer, yellowhammer.

–ahr-**muhr**

(2) armor, charmer, farmer. (3) snake charmer.

–ee-**muhr**

(2) dreamer, emir, femur, lemur, reamer, schemer, steamer, streamer. (3) blasphemer, redeemer.

–eh-**muhr**

(2) hemmer, tremor. (3) condemner, contemnor.

–i-**muhr**

(2) dimmer, glimmer, grimmer, primer, primmer, shimmer, simmer, skimmer, slimmer, swimmer, trimmer.

–oh-**muhr**

(2) comber, homer, Homer, omer, roamer. (3) beachcomber, misnomer.

–ohr-**muhr**

(2) dormer, former, warmer. (3) barnstormer, brainstormer, conformer, informer, performer, reformer, transformer.

–oo-**muhr**

(2) bloomer, boomer, humor, rumor, tumor. (3) consumer, perfumer.

–uh-**muhr**

(2) comer, drummer, dumber, hummer, mummer, plumber, summer. (3) late-comer, midsummer, newcomer.

–uhr-**muhr**

(2) firmer, murmur, termer. (2) affirmer, confirmer.

–aa-**nuhr**

(2) banner, canner, manner, manor, planner, scanner, spanner, tanner.

–ah-**nuhr**

(2) goner, honor, wanner. (3) dishonor. (4) marathoner.

–ay-**nuhr**

(2) drainer, gainer, plainer, saner, strainer, trainer. (3) abstainer, campaigner, chicaner, complainer, container, profaner, retainer. (4) entertainer.

–ee-**nuhr**

(2) cleaner, gleaner, greener, meaner, wiener. (3) demeanor. (4) misdemeanor.

–eh-**nuhr**

(2) tenor. (4) countertenor, heldentenor.

–ei-**nuhr**

(2) diner, finer, liner, miner, minor, shiner, Shriner, signer, whiner. (3) airliner, assigner, consignor, definer, designer, eyeliner, hard-liner, jetliner, one-liner, recliner, refiner. (4) Asia Minor, forty-niner, party-liner, Ursa Minor.

–i-**nuhr**

(2) dinner, grinner, inner, pinner, sinner, skinner, spinner, tinner, winner. (3) beginner, muleskinner.

–oh-**nuhr**

(2) boner, donor, droner, groaner, loaner, loner, moaner, owner, toner. (3) atoner, condoner, intoner, landowner.

–ohr-**nuhr**

(2) corner, mourner, scorner. (3) adorner, suborner.

–oo-**nuhr**

(2) crooner, lunar, pruner, schooner, sooner, swooner, tuner. (3) harpooner, impugner, lacunar, oppugner. (4) importuner.

–oy-**nuhr**

(2) coiner, joiner. (3) enjoiner, purloiner.

–uhr-**nuhr**

(2) burner, earner, learner, turner. (3) sojourner.

–aa-**puhr**

(2) capper, clapper, crapper, dapper, flapper, sapper, trapper, wrapper, zapper. (3) entrapper, fly-sapper, kidnapper. (4) handicapper, understrapper, wiretapper, whippersnapper.

–aam-**puhr**

(2) camper, damper, hamper, pamper, scamper, stamper, tamper, tramper.

–aas-**puhr**

(2) Casper, gasper, jasper, Jasper.

–ah-**puhr**

(2) chopper, copper, cropper, hopper, popper, proper, shopper, stopper, topper, whopper. (3) clodhopper, eavesdropper, grasshopper, improper, namedropper, sharecropper, showstopper. (4) window-shopper.

–ay-**puhr**

(2) caper, draper, paper, taper, tapir, vapor. (3) flypaper, landscaper, newspaper, sandpaper, skyscraper, wallpaper.

–ee-**puhr**

(2) beeper, cheaper, creeper, deeper, keeper, leaper, peeper, reaper, sleeper, steeper, sweeper. (3) beekeeper, bookkeeper, gatekeeper, housekeeper, innkeeper, shopkeeper, zookeeper.

–eh-**puhr**

(2) leper, pepper, stepper. (3) high-stepper.

–ei-**puhr**

(2) diaper, griper, piper, riper, sniper, striper, viper, wiper.
(3) bagpiper, pied piper, sandpiper. (4) windshield wiper.

–i-**puhr**

(2) chipper, clipper, dipper, flipper, gypper, kipper, nipper, shipper, sipper, skipper, slipper, snipper, stripper, tipper, tripper, whipper.
(3) Yom Kippur.

–im-**puhr**

(2) crimper, limper, simper, whimper.

–is-**puhr**

(2) crisper, lisper, whisper.

–oo-**puhr**

(2) blooper, cooper, grouper, hooper, pooper, snooper, stupor, super, trouper, whooper. (4) pooper-scooper, super-duper.

–oh-**puhr**

(2) groper, roper, toper. (3) eloper. (4) interloper.

–ohr-**puhr**

(2) torpor, warper.

–uh-**puhr**

(2) crupper, scupper, supper, upper.

–uhm-**puhr**

(2) bumper, dumper, jumper, plumper, pumper, stumper, thumper.

–uhr-**puhr**

(2) chirper. (3) usurper.

–aan-**suhr**

(2) answer, cancer, Cancer, dancer, lancer, prancer, Prancer.
(3) advancer, enhancer, freelancer, merganser, romancer.
(4) chiromancer, geomancer, necromancer.

–eh-**suhr**

(2) dresser, guesser, lesser, lessor, presser. (3) addresser, aggressor, assessor, compressor, confessor, depressor, oppressor, possessor, professor, successor, suppressor, transgressor. (4) antecessor, intercessor, predecessor, second-guesser, tongue-depressor.

–ehn-**suhr**

(2) censer, censor, denser, fencer, Spencer, sensor, tensor.
(3) commencer, condenser, dispenser, extensor.

–ik-**suhr**

(2) fixer, mixer. (3) elixir.

–oh-suhr

(2) closer, grocer, grosser.

–uhr-suhr

(2) bursar, cursor, mercer, purser. (3) disburser, precursor.

–aa-shuhr

(2) Asher, basher, Dasher, flasher, masher, rasher, slasher, thrasher. (3) gatecrasher. (4) haberdasher, party crasher.

–aap-shuhr

(2) capture, rapture. (3) enrapture, recapture.

–ah-shuhr

(2) josher, washer.

–eh-shuhr

(2) fresher, pressure, thresher. (3) refresher.

–i-shuhr

(2) fisher, fissure, swisher, wisher. (3) kingfisher, well-wisher.

–uh-shuhr

(2) blusher, brusher, crusher, flusher, gusher, plusher, rusher, usher.

–aa-stuhr

(2) aster, Astor, blaster, caster, castor, faster, master, pastor, plaster, vaster. (3) bandmaster, cadastre, disaster, forecaster, headmaster, ringmaster, schoolmaster, spymaster, taskmaster. (4) alabaster, burgomaster, concertmaster, criticaster, overmaster, poetaster, quartermaster, Zoroaster.

–ah-stuhr (–aw-stuhr)

(2) foster, roster. (3) imposter. (4) paternoster.

–ahb-stuhr

(2) lobster, mobster.

–ay-stuhr

(2) baster, taster, waster.

–ee-stuhr

(2) Easter, feaster. (3) nor'easter.

–in-stuhr

(2) minster, spinster. (3) Westminster.

–oh-stuhr

(2) boaster, coaster, poster, roaster, toaster. (3) four-poster. (4) roller coaster.

–ohl-stuhr

(2) bolster, holster. (3) upholster.

–oy-stuhr

(2) cloister, hoister, moister, oyster, roister.

–uh-stuhr

(2) bluster, buster, cluster, Custer, duster, fluster, luster, muster, thruster. (3) adjuster, lackluster. (4) filibuster.

–aa-tuhr

(2) attar, batter, chatter, clatter, fatter, flatter, hatter, latter, matter, patter, ratter, satyr, scatter, shatter, smatter, spatter, splatter, tatter. (3) Mad Hatter.

–aaf-tuhr

(2) after, dafter, drafter, grafter, laughter, rafter. (3) hereafter, thereafter. (4) hereinafter.

–aak-tuhr

(2) actor, factor, tractor. (3) abstractor, attractor, compactor, contractor, detractor, distracter, enactor, exactor, extractor, protractor, refractor, retractor. (4) benefactor, malefactor.

–aan-tuhr

(2) banter, canter, cantor, chanter, grantor, planter. (3) decanter, descanter, enchanter, implanter.

–aap-tuhr

(2) captor, chapter. (3) adapter.

–ah-tuhr

(2) blotter, cottar, cotter, daughter, dotter, hotter, jotter, otter, plotter, potter, slaughter, squatter, spotter, swatter, totter, trotter, water. (3) complotter, manslaughter. (4) alma mater.

–ahk-**tuhr**

(2) doctor, proctor. (3) concocter.

–ahp-**tuhr**

(2) copter. (3) adopter. (4) helicopter.

–ahr-**tuhr**

(2) barter, carter, charter, darter, garter, martyr, starter, tartar.
(3) non-starter, self-starter.

–aw-**tuhr**

(2) daughter, slaughter, tauter, water. (3) backwater, dishwater, granddaughter, manslaughter, rainwater, rosewater, stepdaughter.

–awl-**tuhr**

(2) altar, alter, falter, halter, palter, vaulter, Walter. (3) assaulter, defaulter, exalter, Gibraltar, unalter.

–awn-**tuhr**

(2) flaunter, gaunter, haunter, saunter.

–ay-**tuhr**

(2) cater, crater, freighter, gaiter, gator, grater, greater, later, satyr, tater, traitor, waiter. (3) creator, curator, Decatur, dictator, dumbwaiter, equator, spectator, testator. (4) alligator, carburetor, commentator, conservator, elevator, fascinator, gladiator.
ALSO: Words created by addition of suffixes –er and –or
(i.e., *skater*, *investigator*).

–ayn-**tuhr**

(2) fainter, painter, tainter.

–ee-**tuhr**

(2) beater, cheater, eater, greeter, heater, liter, meter, neater, Peter, praetor, sweeter, tweeter. (3) beefeater, Demeter, eggbeater, fire-eater, man-eater, repeater, saltpeter, centimeter, decimeter, hexameter, kilometer, lotus-eater, millimeter, overeater, space heater.

–eh-**tuhr**

(2) better, bettor, debtor, fetter, getter, letter, setter, wetter.
(3) abettor, begetter, forgetter, go-getter, newsletter, pacesetter, red-letter, typesetter, unfetter.

–ehk-tuhr

(2) hector, Hector, lector, nectar, rector, sector, specter, vector. (3) collector, convector, defector, deflector, detector, director, ejector, elector, injector, inspector, objector, projector, prospector, protector, reflector, selector.

–ehl-tuhr

(2) pelter, shelter, smelter, spelter, swelter, welter. (4) helter-skelter.

–ehn-tuhr

(2) center, enter, mentor, renter. (3) dead-center, dissenter, frequenter, inventor, lamenter, off-center, precentor, presenter, re-enter, repenter, tormentor. (4) epicenter. (5) experimenter.

–ehs-tuhr

(2) Chester, ester, Esther, fester, jester, Lester, Nestor, pester, tester, wrester. (3) digester, Dorchester, investor, Manchester, nor'wester, protester, Rochester, semester, sequester, Sylvester, trimester, Westchester. (4) empty-nester, polyester.

–ei-tuhr

(2) biter, blighter, brighter, fighter, lighter, miter, niter, tighter, titer, triter, writer. (3) backbiter, first-nighter, igniter, inciter, indicter, moonlighter, speechwriter, prizefighter, typewriter. (4) copyrighter, copywriter, dynamiter, underwriter. (5) paperback writer.

–i-tuhr

(2) bitter, fitter, flitter, fritter, glitter, hitter, jitter, knitter, litter, pitter, quitter, sitter, spitter, splitter, titter, twitter. (3) atwitter, committer, embitter, transmitter. (4) babysitter, counterfeiter.

–if-tuhr

(2) drifter, grifter, lifer, shifter, sifter, swifter. (3) shape-shifter, shoplifter.

–ik-tuhr

(2) lictor, stricter, victor. (3) afflicter, constrictor, inflictor, predictor. (4) contradictor, boa constrictor, vasoconstrictor.

–il-tuhr

(2) filter, jilter, kilter, philter, quilter. (3) off-kilter.

–in-tuhr

(2) hinter, minter, printer, splinter, sprinter, squinter, stinter, tinter, winter.

–is-tuhr

(2) bistre, blister, glister, mister, sister, twister. (3) insister, persister, resister, transistor.

–oh-tuhr

(2) boater, bloater, doter, floater, motor, quoter, rotor, voter.
(3) promoter.

–ohl-tuhr

(2) bolter, coulter, jolter. (3) revolter.

–ohr-tuhr

(2) mortar, porter, quarter, shorter, snorter, sorter. (3) distorter, exporter, extorter, importer, reporter, ripsnorter, supporter.

–oo-tuhr

(2) cuter, hooter, looter, neuter, pewter, rooter, scooter, tutor.
(3) commuter, computer, disputer, freebooter, polluter, recruiter, refuter. (4) coadjutor, prosecutor.

–ow-tuhr

(2) doubter, flouter, pouter, router, shouter, stouter, touter.

–own-tuhr

(2) counter, mounter. (3) discounter, encounter.

–oy-tuhr

(2) goiter, loiter. (3) exploiter, (4) reconnoiter.

–oyn-tuhr

(2) jointer, pointer. (3) anointer.

–uh-tuhr

(2) butter, clutter, cutter, flutter, gutter, mutter, putter, shutter, splutter, sputter, strutter, stutter, utter. (3) abutter, rebutter, stonecutter, woodcutter.

–uhk-tuhr

(3) abductor, adductor, conductor, constructor, obstructor.
(4) nonconductor. (5) semiconductor.

–uhn-tuhr

(2) blunter, bunter, grunter, hunter, punter. (3) confronter.

–uhr-tuhr

(2) blurter, curter, flirter, hurter, squirter. (3) asserter, averter, converter, deserter, diverter, inserter, inverter, subverter.

–aa-thuhr

(2) blather, gather, lather, rather, slather. (3) foregather.

–ah-thuhr

(2) bother, father, pother.

–ee-thuhr

(2) breather, either, neither.

–eh-thuhr

(2) blether, feather, heather, leather, nether, tether, weather, whether. (3) bellwether, pinfeather, together, whitleather. (4) altogether, get-together.

–ei-thuhr

(2) blither, either, lither, neither, tither, writher.

–i-thuhr

(2) blither, dither, hither, thither, slither, whither, wither, zither.

–uh-thuhr

(2) brother, mother, other, smother. (3) another.

–aan-thhuhr

(2) anther, panther.

–aa-vuhr

(3) cadaver, palaver.

–ahl-vuhr

(2) solver. (3) absolver, dissolver, evolver, resolver, revolver.

–ay-vuhr

(2) braver, craver, favor, flavor, graver, quaver, savor, shaver, slaver, waiver, waver. (3) disfavor, engraver, enslaver, lifesaver, timesaver.

–ee-**vuhr**

(2) beaver, cleaver, fever, griever, leaver, reaver, reiver, weaver.
(3) achiever, believer, conceiver, deceiver, receiver. (4) cantilever,
non-believer, unbeliever. (5) overachiever, underachiever.

–eh-**vuhr**

(2) clever, ever, lever, never, sever, Trevor. (3) dissever, en-
deavor, however, whatever, whenever, wherever, whichever,
whoever, whomever. (4) howsoever, whatsoever, whencesoever,
wheresoever, whomsoever, whosesoever, whosoever.

–ei-**vuhr**

(2) diver, driver, fiver, skiver. (3) conniver, contriver, deriver,
reviver, survivor.

–i-**vuhr**

(2) flivver, giver, liver, quiver, river, shiver, sliver. (3) deliver,
forgiver.

–oh-**vuhr**

(2) clover, Dover, drover, over, plover, rover, stover, trover.
(3) crossover, flyover, hangover, Hanover, leftover, moreover,
Passover, pullover, pushover, stopover.

–uh-**vuhr**

(2) cover, lover, plover, shover. (3) discover, recover, uncover.

–uhr-**vuhr**

(2) fervor, server. (3) conserver, observer, preserver.

–ayv-**yuhr**

(2) savior. (3) behavior. (4) misbehavior.

–ay-**zuhr**

(2) blazer, gazer, laser, maser, phaser, raiser, razor. (3) appraiser,
fundraiser, hell-raiser, stargazer, trailblazer.

–ee-**zuhr**

(2) Caesar, easer, freezer, geezer, pleaser, sneezer, squeezer, teaser,
tweezer, wheezer. (3) Crowd-pleaser. (4) Ebenezer, people-pleaser.

–ei-zuhr

(2) geyser, kaiser, miser, sizar, visor, wiser. (3) adviser, divisor, incisor. (4) appetizer, atomizer, energizer, fertilizer, supervisor.
ALSO: **–eiz** + *-er* (i.e., *chastiser*, *equalizer*).

–i-zuhr

(2) quizzer, scissor, whizzer.

–oo-zuhr

(2) boozer, bruiser, chooser, cruiser, loser, user. (3) abuser, accuser, amuser, diffuser, excuser.

–ow-zuhr

(2) browser, dowser, rouser, schnauzer, trouser. (3) carouser.
(4) rabble-rouser.

–ay-zhuhr

(2) brazier, glazier.

–eh-zhuhr

(2) leisure, measure, pleasure, treasure. (3) admeasure, displeasure, entreasure, outmeasure. (4) countermeasure.

–oh-zhuhr

(2) closure, crosier, hosier, osier. (3) composure, disclosure, enclosure, exposure, foreclosure. (4) discomposure.

–uhrch

(1) birch, church, lurch, perch, search, smirch. (2) besmirch, research.

–uhrd

(1) bird, curd, gird, heard, herd, Kurd, nerd, purred, surd, third, turd, word. (2) absurd, blackbird, bluebird, foreword, lovebird, songbird, unheard. (3) hummingbird, ladybird, mockingbird, overheard.
ALSO: **–ur** + *-ed* (i.e., *slurred*, *occurred*).

–oo-uhrd

(2) leeward, sewered, skewered, steward.

–ow-uhrd

(2) coward, cowered, floured, flowered, Howard, powered, showered, towered. (3) high-powered.

–aa-**buhrd**

(2) clapboard, jabbered, scabbard, tabard.

–ahr-**buhrd**

(2) barbered, harbored, larboard, starboard.

–uh-**buhrd**

(2) blubbered, cupboard, Hubbard.

–ohr-**chuhrd**

(2) orchard, tortured.

–aa-**guhrd**

(2) blackguard, haggard, laggard, staggered, swaggered.

–i-**guhrd**

(2) jiggered, niggard.

–aang-**kuhrd**

(2) anchored, cankered, hankered, tankard.

–uhng-**kuhrd**

(2) bunkered, drunkard.

–ah-**luhrd**

(2) bollard, pollard.

–eh-**puhrd**

(2) jeopard, leopard, peppered, shepherd.

–aas-**tuhrd**

(2) bastard, dastard, mastered, plastered.

–uhs-**tuhrd**

(2) blustered, bustard, clustered, custard, flustered, mustard, mustered.

–il-**yuhrd**

(2) billiard, milliard.

–aa-**zuhrd**

(2) hazard. (3) haphazard.

–i-**zuhrd**

(2) blizzard, gizzard, izzard, lizard, scissored, vizard, wizard.

–uhrb

(1) blurb, curb, herb, Serb, verb. (2) acerb, adverb, disturb, perturb, suburb, superb.

–uhrf

(1) scurf, serf, smurf, surf, turf.

–uhrg

(1) berg, burgh. (2) iceberg.

–uhrj

(1) dirge, merge, purge scourge, serge, splurge, spurge, surge, urge, verge. (2) converge, deterge, diverge, emerge, immerge, submerge. (3) demiurge, dramaturge.

–uhrk

(1) burke, cirque, clerk, dirk, Dirk, irk, jerk, Kirk, lurk, murk, perk, quirk, shirk, smirk, Turk, work. (2) artwork, berserk, bridgework, Dunkirk, guesswork, homework, housework, rework. (3) busywork, handiwork, masterwork, overwork, soda jerk.

–uhrl

(1) burl, churl, curl, earl, Earl, furl, girl, hurl, knurl, pearl, purl, swirl, twirl, whirl, whorl. (2) uncurl, unfurl.

–uhrld

(1) whorled, world. (2) new-world, old-world. (3) Netherworld, other-world, underworld.

–uhrm

(1) firm, germ, sperm, squirm, term, worm. (2) affirm, bookworm, confirm, glowworm, infirm. (3) isotherm, pachyderm, reaffirm.

–uhrn

(1) Berne, burn, churn, earn, erne, fern, kern, learn, quern, spurn, stern, tern, turn, urn, yearn. (2) adjourn, astern, concern, discern, eterne, intern, Lucerne, nocturne, return, sojourn, unlearn. (3) overturn, taciturn, unconcern.

–aa-**tuhrn**

(2) pattern, Saturn, slattern.

–aa-**vuhrn**

(2) cavern, tavern.

–uhrp

(1) burp, chirp, slurp, twerp, urp. (2) usurp.

–uhrs

(1) curse, Erse, hearse, nurse, purse, terse, verse, worse. (2) accurse, adverse, amerce, asperse, averse, coerce, commerce, converse, disburse, disperse, diverse, immerse, inverse, obverse, perverse, rehearse, reverse, traverse, transverse. (3) intersperse, reimburse, universe.

–uhrst

(1) burst, curst, durst, erst, first, Hearst, thirst, worst. (2) knackwurst, outburst, sunburst. (3) liverwurst.
ALSO: **–urs** + *-ed* (i.e., *cursed, reversed*).

–uhrt

(1) Bert, blurt, Burt, curt, dirt, flirt, Gert, girt, hurt, Kurt, pert, shirt, skirt, spurt, squirt. (2) advert, Albert, alert, assert, avert, concert, convert, covert, desert, dessert, divert, exert, expert, filbert, Herbert, inert, insert, invert, overt, pervert, revert, subvert, T-shirt, unhurt. (3) controvert, disconcert, extrovert, introvert.

–uhrth

(1) berth, birth, dearth, earth, firth, girth, mirth, Perth, worth.
(2) stillbirth, unearth.

–uhrv

(1) curve, Irv, nerve, oeuvre, serve, swerve, verve. (2) conserve, deserve, hors d'oeuvre, incurve, innerve, observe, preserve, reserve, unnerve.

–uhs

(1) bus, buss, cuss, fuss, Gus, muss, plus, pus, Russ, thus, truss, us.
(2) cirrus, nimbus, nonplus, Remus, stratus, Taurus, Venus. (3) abacus, Angelus, animus, cumulus, exodus, impetus, incubus, minibus, nautilus, octopus, Oedipus, omnibus, Pegasus, platypus, Priapus, radius, Romulus, Sirius, stimulus, succubus, Tantalus, terminus, Uranus.
(4) Aquarius, esophagus, homunculus, Leviticus, sarcophagus.
(5) Sagittarius.
ALSO: Words created with addition of suffix *-ous* (i.e., *dangerous*).

–ay-nee-uhs

(4) cutaneous, extraneous, spontaneous. (5) instantaneous, miscellaneous, simultaneous. (6) contemporaneous, extemporaneous.

–ee-vee-uhs

(3) devious, previous.

–ehr-uhs

(2) Paris, harass. (3) embarrass, Polaris.

–ehr-ee-uhs

(2) Darius, various. (3) Aquarius, gregarious, hilarious, nefarious, precarious, vicarious. (4) multifarious, Sagittarius, temerarious.

–ei-uhs

(2) bias, pious.

–ohr-uhs

(2) Boris, chorus, Doris, loris, Horace, Morris, Norris, porous, Taurus, torus. (3) decorous, pylorus, sonorous. (4) brontosaurus, stegosaurus.

–ah-duhs

(2) bodice, goddess.

–ehn-duhs

(2) horrendous, stupendous, tremendous.

–ay-juhs

(3) contagious, courageous, outrageous, rampageous, umbrageous.
(4) advantageous. (5) disadvantageous.

–i-juhs

(3) litigious, prodigious, religious. (4) irreligious, sacrilegious.

–is-**kuhs**

(2) discus, viscous. (3) hibiscus, meniscus.

–oh-**kuhs**

(2) crocus, focus, hocus, locus. (4) hocus-pocus.

–aap-**luhs**

(2) hapless, sapless, strapless.

–ahrm-**luhs**

(2) armless, charmless, harmless.

–eh-**luhs**

(2) Hellas, jealous, trellis, zealous. (3) entellus, Marcellus.

–ehk-**luhs**

(2) feckless, fleckless, necklace, reckless, speckless.

–oothh-**luhs**

(2) ruthless, toothless, truthless.

–ay-**muhs**

(2) Amos, famous, shamus. (3) biramous, mandamus. (4) ignoramus.

–is-**muhs**

(2) Christmas, isthmus.

–oo-**muhs**

(2) hummus, spumous.

–aad-**nuhs**

(2) badness, gladness, madness, sadness.

–eh-**nuhs**

(2) Dennis, menace, tenace, tennis, Venice.

–ei-**nuhs**

(2) dryness, highness, Linus, Minos, minus, shyness, sinus, slyness, spinous, vinous, wryness. (3) Aquinas, echinus. (4) Your Highness.

–oh-**nuhs**

(2) bonus, Cronus, Jonas, onus, slowness. (3) colonus.

–aam-**puhs**

(2) campus, grampus, pampas. (3) hippocampus.

–uhm-**puhs**

(2) compass, rumpus. (3) encompass.

–ei-**ruhs**

(2) Cyrus, iris, virus. (3) desirous, Osiris, papyrus.

–ay-**suhs**

(2) basis, glacis, phases, stasis. (3) oasis.

–ee-**suhs**

(2) rhesus, thesis. (3) kinesis, mimesis, prothesis. (4) anamnesis, catachresis, exegesis. (5) hyperkinesis, telekinesis. (6) amniocentesis, aposiopesis.

–ehk-**suhs**

(2) nexus, plexus, Texas. (3) Alexis. (4) solar plexus.

–ei-**suhs**

(2) crisis, Isis, phthisis.

–aw-**shuhs**

(2) cautious, nauseous. (3) precautious.

–ay-**shuhs**

(2) gracious, spacious. (3) audacious, bulbaceous, capacious, cetaceous, cretaceous, crustaceous, edacious, fallacious, flirtatious, fugacious, herbaceous, Ignatius, lardaceous, loquacious, mendacious, mordacious, predaceous, pugnacious, rapacious, sagacious, salacious, sebaceous, setaceous, tenacious, ungracious, veracious, vexatious, vivacious, voracious. (4) alliaceous, capillaceous, carbonaceous, contumacious, disputatious, efficacious, erinaceous, farinaceous, ferulaceous, liliaceous, orchidaceous, ostentatious, perspicacious, pertinacious, saponaceous. (5) inefficacious.

–ee-**shuhs**

(2) specious. (3) capricious, facetious, pernicious.

–ehn-**shuhs**

(3) abstentious, contentious, dissentious, licentious, pretentious, sententious, tendentious. (4) conscientious, unpretentious.

–i-shuhs

(2) vicious. (3) ambitious, auspicious, capricious, delicious, factitious, judicious, lubricious, malicious, nutritious, officious, pernicious, propitious, seditious, suspicious. (4) avaricious, expeditious, inauspicious, injudicious, meretricious, superstitious, supposititious, surreptitious.

–oh-shuhs

(3) atrocious, ferocious, precocious.

–uhmp-shuhs

(2) bumptious, scrumptious. (3) presumptuous.

–aa-tuhs

(2) gratis, lattice, status, stratus. (3) clematis. (4) apparatus.

–aak-tuhs

(2) cactus, practice. (3) malpractice.

–ay-tuhs

(2) status. (3) afflatus, hiatus.

–ee-tuhs

(2) fetus, Thetis, treatise. (3) boletus, coitus, quietus.

–it-nuhs

(2) fitness, witness.

–il-yuhs

(2) bilious. (3) punctilious. (4) atrabilious, supercilious.

–uhsk

(1) brusque, busk, dusk, husk, musk, rusk, tusk.

–uhst

(1) bussed, bust, cussed, crust, dost, dust, fussed, gust, just, lust, mussed, must, rust, thrust, trussed, trust. (2) adjust, august, August, combust, disgust, distrust, encrust, entrust, incrust, mistrust, nonplussed, piecrust, robust, stardust, unjust. (3) antitrust, wanderlust.

–uht

(1) but, butt, cut, glut, gut, hut, jut, mutt, nut, putt, rut, shut, slut, smut, strut, what. (2) abut, beechnut, catgut, chestnut, clear-cut, crewcut, haircut, King Tut, peanut, rebut, rotgut, shortcut, uncut, walnut. (3) betelnut, butternut, coconut, halibut, hazelnut, scuttlebutt, undercut, uppercut.

–ehr-uht

(2) carat, caret, carrot, claret, ferret, garret, karat, merit, parrot.
(3) demerit, inherit. (4) disinherit.

–ei-uht

(2) diet, fiat, quiet, riot, striate. (3) disquiet.

–oo-uht

(2) bluet, cruet, suet. (3) intuit.

–aa-buht

(2) abbot, habit, rabbet, rabbit. (3) cohabit, inhabit, jackrabbit.

–aam-buht

(2) ambit, gambit.

–i-buht

(2) gibbet. (3) exhibit, inhibit, prohibit.

–aa-chuht

(2) hatchet, latchet, ratchet.

–aan-duht

(2) bandit, pandit.

–aw-duht

(2) audit, plaudit.

–aa-guht

(2) agate, faggot, fagot, maggot.

–i-guht

(2) bigot, frigate, gigot, spigot.

–id-juht

(2) Bridget, digit, fidget, Gidget, midget.

–aa-kuht

(2) bracket, jacket, packet, placket, racket. (3) straightjacket, yellow-jacket.

–ah-kuht

(2) brocket, Crockett, docket, locket, pocket, rocket, socket, sprocket. (3) pick-pocket, skyrocket.

–i-kuht

(2) cricket, picket, piquet, pricket, thicket, ticket, wicket.

–is-kuht

(2) biscuit, brisket.

–uh-kuht

(2) bucket, tucket. (3) Nantucket, Pawtucket.

–aa-luht

(2) ballot, mallet, palate, pallet, palette, shallot.

–aam-luht

(2) camlet, hamlet, Hamlet, samlet.

–ahr-luht

(2) harlot, scarlet, starlet, varlet.

–eh-luht

(2) helot, pellet, prelate, zealot.

–ei-luht

(2) eyelet, islet, pilot.

–i-luht

(2) billet, fillet, millet, rillet, skillet.

–ib-luht

(2) driblet, giblet, gimlet.

–oop-luht

(2) drupelet. (3) quadruplet, quintuplet, septuplet, sextuplet.

–uh-luht

(2) cullet, gullet, mullet.

–uu-luht

(2) bullet, pullet.

–uh-muht

(2) plummet, summit.

–aa-nuht

(2) gannet, granite, Janet, planet. (3) pomegranate.

–ah-nuht

(2) bonnet, sonnet.

–eh-nuht

(2) Bennett, jennet, rennet, senate, tenet.

–i-nuht

(2) linnet, minute, spinet.

–ohr-nuht

(2) cornet, hornet.

–aa-puht

(2) lappet, tappet.

–i-puht

(2) sippet, snippet, tippet, whippet.

–uhm-puht

(2) crumpet, strumpet, trumpet.

–aa-suht

(2) asset, basset, facet, tacit.

–aan-suht

(2) lancet, transit. (4) Narragansett.

–uh-suht

(2) gusset, russet.

–i-vuht

(2) civet, divot, pivot, privet, rivet, trivet.

–ah-zuht

(2) closet, posit. (3) deposit.

–uhv

(1) dove, glove, love, of, shove. (2) above, foxglove, hereof, thereof, true love, whereof. (3) ladylove, turtledove.

–uhz

(1) buzz, coz, does, fuzz.

–aa-suhz

(2) asses, classes, glasses, lasses, masses, molasses, passes. (3) amasses, harasses, surpasses. (4) overpasses, underpasses.

–uud

(1) could, good, hood, should, stood, wood, would. (2) childhood, firewood, manhood, monkshood, withstood. (3) babyhood, brotherhood, fatherhood, hardihood, likelihood, livelihood, maidenhood, motherhood, neighborhood, parenthood, Robin Hood, sandalwood, sisterhood, understood, womanhood. (4) misunderstood.

–ah-lee-wud

(3) Bollywood, Dollywood, Hollywood.

–uuf

(1) hoof, woof.

–uuk

(1) book, brook, cook, crook, hook, look, nook, rook, shook, took. (2) betook, Chinook, forsook, mistook, outlook, partook. (3) overlook, pocketbook, undertook.

–uul

(1) bull, full, pull, wool. (2) capful, cupful, final, graceful, lambswool, mogul. (3) beautiful, bountiful, dutiful, fanciful, Istanbul, masterful, merciful, pitiful, plentiful, powerful, Sitting Bull, sorrowful, teaspoonful, wonderful, worshipful. (4) tablespoonful.

–uur

(1) boor, cure, moor, poor, pure, spoor, tour, your, you're. (2) abjure, adjure, allure, amour, assure, brochure, cocksure, coiffeur, contour, demure, detour, endure, ensure, immure, impure, injure, insure, inure, manure, mature, obscure, ordure, procure, secure, unsure. (3) amateur, aperture, armature, cynosure, epicure, forfeiture, furniture, immature, insecure, ligature, overture, paramour, portraiture, premature, reassure, signature, sinecure, troubadour. (4) caricature, expenditure, investiture, literature, miniature, musculature, nomenclature, temperature. (5) primogeniture.

–uush

(1) bush, push, shush, squoosh, swoosh, tush. (2) ambush, Hindu Kush.

–uut

(1) foot, put, soot. (2) afoot, forefoot, hotfoot, input, output. (3) pussyfoot, tenderfoot, underfoot.